WADDESDON'S
GOLDEN YEARS
1874–1925

NORMAN CARR & IVOR GURNEY

ISBN 0-9547310-0-X

Published in aid of Waddesdon Village Hall

Published by The Alice Trust, Waddesdon Manor
Produced by Sutton Publishing Ltd, Stroud, Gloucestershire
First printed 1996 in Great Britain by Henry Lings Ltd, Dorchester
Reprinted in Great Britain by Butler & Tanner, Frome, Somerset.

CONTENTS

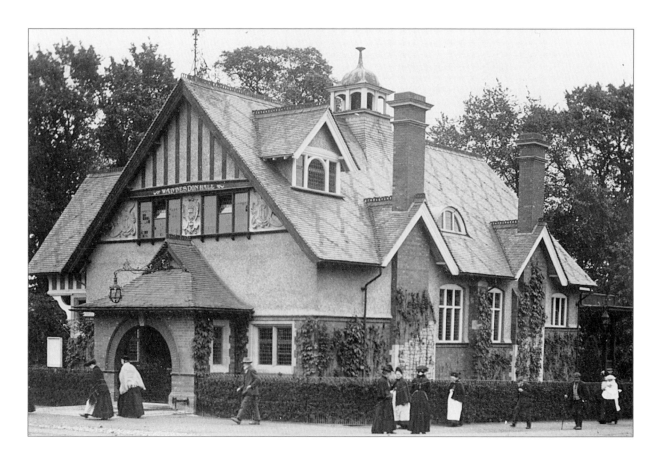

One hundred years old in 1997, Waddesdon's splendid Village Hall was built by Baron Ferdinand de Rothschild as a venue for the wide variety of uplifting social activities which flourished in the village. Until 1968 this hall was run and maintained by the Waddesdon Estate. In 1968 ownership was transferred to a Charitable Trust, and the hall became self-financing. The running of the hall, its maintenance and improvement programmes are the responsibility of the Management Committee, which comprises appointees from the trustees, village organisations and co-opted persons. Income is mainly derived from lettings and fund-raising events.

FOREWORD

In their excellent and interesting book on Waddesdon's Golden Years, Norman Carr and Ivor Gurney pay a great compliment to Baron Ferdinand de Rothschild by making 1874, the year when he acquired the Waddesdon Estate from the Duke of Marlborough, the starting point for their book about "the Golden Years". The compliment is a well-deserved one. When the Baron died suddenly at the age of 59 in 1898 the *Morning Leader*, in their obituary, wrote "The grief in Waddesdon is most touching, the death of a great landed proprietor always casts gloom into the village which was dependent on him, but Baron Rothschild was far more to Waddesdon than merely a great landowner and employer. Waddesdon knew it had lost the best friend it had ever had."

One instance is sufficient to show what sort of a man the Baron was. He was himself a tee-totaller but knew that others were not and realised that men who did not think as he did liked to meet at the village inn. He built one for them, the Five Arrows, and furnished it. It is a little mansion, as pretty as a picture. He helped to design it himself.

His great fear was that, with no descendants, Waddesdon might fall into decay and he ended his Red Book about the Manor on a worrying note of concern: "May the day be yet distant when weeds will spread over the gardens, and terraces crumble to dust, the pictures and cabinets cross the Channel or Atlantic, and the melancholy cry of the night jar sound from the deserted towers".

However, Miss Alice de Rothschild and then Mr. and Mrs. James de Rothschild cared for his great creations and the traditions of friendship and support for the village that he had set up and now, almost a hundred years after Baron Ferdinand's death, the relationship between the village, the Manor and Estate continues and is as lively and as close as ever. Beer and wine continues to flow in the Five Arrows which Baron Ferdinand had built, and last year the Manor welcomed no less than 150,000 visitors. Waddesdon had become a great tourist attraction, visited from all over the world. Last year a huge tribute was paid to the village of Waddesdon, as well as to the House that Baron Ferdinand had created, when Her Majesty the Queen and His Royal Highness the Duke of Edinburgh visited Waddesdon some 105 years after the visit of Queen Victoria in 1890.

Both these events have been memorably described and photographed in Norman Carr and Ivor Gurney's book and they have succeeded in bringing to life Waddesdon's "Golden Years". I am delighted that the book is available to the growing number of visitors to Waddesdon Manor and all those who share our interest in the village and this great period. I am sure they will rejoice not just at the memories of a "bygone age" but also that the bygone age still in many ways continues and will continue for many, many generations to come.

Rothschild

LORD ROTHSCHILD
8 January 1996

INTRODUCTION

Until 1874 the village of Waddesdon had existed as a large, unremarkable settlement for hundreds of years, with no special claims to fame and few mentions in the history books.

In common with neighbouring villages the population relied upon agriculture for employment, and many had literally lived off the land, even to the extent of living in "dirt houses", as they were known. With the last of the enclosures in 1774 things went down-hill, and from bad to worse in the early 1800s. It was not until after the 1850s that life could be seen to improve a little. By then Waddesdon had an unsavoury reputation which it would take years to lose.

Unlike most other villages in the Vale of Aylesbury, Waddesdon lacked a big house and a resident rich family which could provide steady work and business opportunities to benefit the community. Although the combined Manor of Waddesdon and Over Winchendon had passed from the Earls of Devon, The Black Prince, Henry VIII, and finally to the Duke of Marlborough amongst many other worthies, none had ever resided in Waddesdon, and who could blame them?

In 1874 the executors of the late Duke of Marlborough sold the Waddesdon and Over Winchendon estates to Baron Ferdinand de Rothschild and things began to look up. The Baron transformed this Vale "ugly duckling", and in doing so provided the local populace with a future beyond their most optimistic dreams. They were given opportunities and grasped them with credit, matching benevolence with endeavour, and setting standards in all aspects of village life which are unlikely to be repeated.

Waddesdon's Golden Years focuses mainly upon the viewpoint of the villagers, and with the help of a superb collection of photographs and unique documents we will convey the reader through this period when Waddesdon reigned supreme in the locality.

The book is divided into four sections which record the original village of 1874, the physical transformations wrought as a result of Baron Ferdinand's acquisition, and the rich variety of village life in the period 1874–1925. A fifth section is included as a sequel, providing a brief statement in print and illustrations of the Waddesdon of 1995.

Fortunately the 1870s coincided with the dawn of an era when photography was elevated to an unsurpassed level of professionalism. This book is also a testimony to that art.

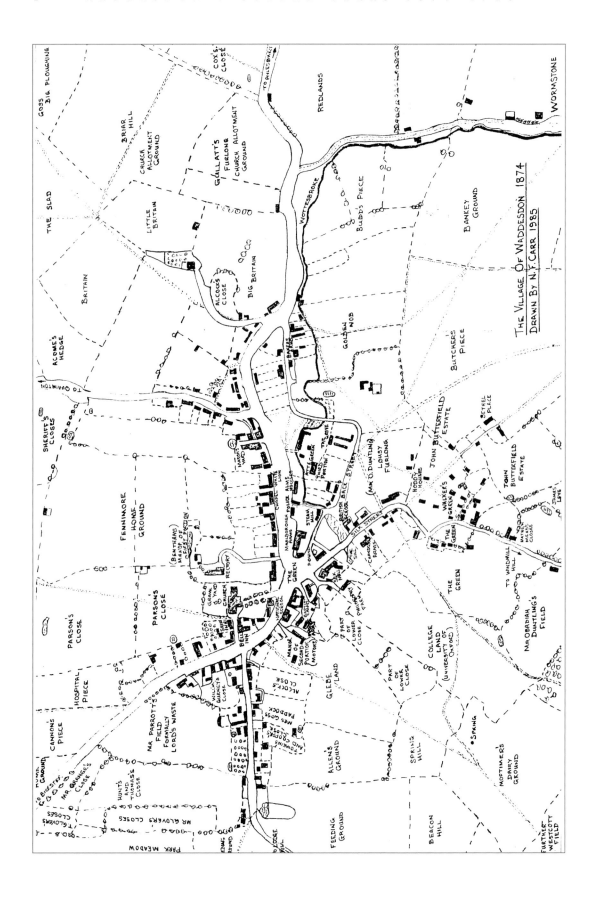

THE VILLAGE BEFORE 1874

This first section shows Waddesdon before Baron Ferdinand's acquisition and gives some idea of a Buckinghamshire village of the period. Although it is thought that all of the photographs were taken after August 1874 most record details which were about to disappear. Others are included to show how little some of the aspects have changed. Both the map and pictorial view taken from Lodge Hill illustrate how the ancient village had gathered around the church, which itself is situated close to the springs and the Wottesbroke flowing from Spring Hill.

At the village centre was the Green, a tiny patch of common land on the junction of Silk Street and High Street. Numerous alleys, lanes and paths connected the unplanned cluster of cottages. These provided homes to a population of around 1,600, a large village by local standards.

Since the loss of common land there had been two main landowners within the parish boundaries, the Church and the Manor. These apart, the only other ownership of note was Philosophy Farm, 339 acres endowed to provide the Sedleian Professorship of Natural Philosophy at Oxford University. Adjacent to many village premises were several small closes of about one acre used for draught horses and domestic livestock.

The community had survived a hundred years of unmitigated hardship. The enclosures, the French Wars, labour-saving agricultural machinery (see sections on Waddesdon charities) and awful living conditions had often combined to sap the morale of the village people. Things had sometimes reached such a low ebb that significant numbers had chosen, with encouragement from the overseers of the poor, to emigrate to America or the colonies. Nonetheless by 1874 there was in Waddesdon evidence of improvement; people were becoming less apathetic, allotments were being cultivated with pride and evening classes were being supported. And now in August interest quickened amongst the tenant farmers and their workers – a new owner had emerged in place of the Duke of Marlborough. Would it make a difference?

1.   This view of Waddesdon taken from Lodge Hill in 1874 shows nearly all the village close by the church on the eastern, southern, and western sides. To the left in this view are Queen Street and Bicester Hill, Silk Street and High Street are to the right with Quainton Road at the right rear. Mr. Taylor's mill chimney can be seen at the extreme right, marking the point where Back Road turned to form the junction with Silk Street. At this time Frederick Street did not exist. In the distance can be seen the smoke from a steam locomotive on the Aylesbury to Claydon line which had been completed six years earlier.

2.   The ancient church of St Michael and All Angels with the Ship Inn on the left and the Bell Inn on the right. Whilst the oldest parts of the church date from around 1190, over the centuries additions and renovations reflect a continuing concern by the villagers to maintain this focal point of community life, and several architectural styles are represented in the building. The distinctive church tower was already becoming dangerous when this photograph was taken, and after a fund-raising campaign it was demolished and rebuilt in 1892. Within the belfry are six steel bells cast by Naylor Vickers and Company of Sheffield, and installed in 1862. The clock bell dates from 1806.

3.   Waddesdon Rectory at Benthams, the Manor of the First Portion. Constructed in 1870 and destined to become the focal point for many village activities in the years to come.

4.   Photographed from a point on the main road opposite the Bell Inn are the terraced cottages which stood alongside the Ship Inn, and the houses on the left were at the crest of Bicester Hill. All these dwellings were of a better standard than most in the village, but were destined for demolition early in the 20th century, making way for "The Cedars". This photograph was taken in 1906, when the householders were, from L to R, Mr. Cripps, Mr. Venemore, Mr. Tommy Wakenell, Mr. Carrick, Mr. Saunders and Mr. Harry Kibble.

The Annual Vestry was held on Thursday, March 24th, the Rector in the chair. There were 20 present. The Overseers', Charity, and Surveyors' accounts were passed. Mr. Edwin Crook was accepted as tenant of the charity ground at Wescott. The following were nominated for the office of Overseers:—Messrs. J. Wood, O. King, Geo. Anthony, Wm. Flowers, J. Rose, J. Goss, J. Crook, R. Adams, T. Matthews, C. Dormer. Messrs. Jos. Crook and J. Rose were chosen to be Surveyors. The subject of the "Alms Cow" was brought before the meeting.

THE RECTORY HOUSE WARMING.

On Feb. 24th, a large party of workmen who had been employed in building the Rectory were, with their employers, Messrs. Anthony, C. Crook, and Joseph Goss (Aylesbury), entertained by the Rector to a good and substantial Supper. The Rector and Mr. James Goss presided, many excellent speeches were made, good wishes exchanged, and a pleasant evening spent. There is great cause for thankfulness that during the work no accident occurred, and the report made by the employers that all the men were uniformly well conducted added not a little to the satisfaction felt by all at the conclusion of the work. It will be remembered that the Corner-stone was laid on July 31st, 1868, by the Ven. Archdeacon Bickersteth, when a special service was held on the ground, followed by a tea in the schoolroom, and a service in the parish church. Some of our readers may like to have the hymn used on that occasion (composed by Mr. W. White, the Architect), and so we have inserted it here.

By Thee, O precious Corner Stone,
The heart's meet dwelling-place alone;
This dwelling-place be bless'd,
Of Thee alone possess'd.

This goodly Corner Stone be laid,
Whilst we invoke the Father's aid
Our handy work to guide,
And in us to abide.

Safe from the toil of earthly strife,
Pure from the stain of earthly life,
Thy Pastor's pathway keep
Within thy mercy's deep.

And from beneath this sacred roof
May evil ever flee aloof;
Nor man, nor friend molest
Thy watchful servants' rest.

This door the holy portal prove,
Whence gentle spirits lightly move
To deeds of faith and love,
As angels from above.

From want and wasting care defend
Thy faithful stewards to the end;
This hearth the altar be
Of burning charity.

And let Elijah's mantle fall,
On prophet, priest, and teachers, all
Who with thy spirit strive
To keep this flame alive.

Men then the praises shall rehearse
Of Thee who built the universe,
Creator, Spirit, Son,
Whilst endless ages run.

WADDESDON NATIONAL SCHOOL ACCOUNT, 1869.

RECEIPTS.	£	s.	d.	EXPENSES.	£	s.	d.
Duke of Marlborough, K.G...	25	0	0	Balance due to Treasurer ..	2	15	4¼
Comte d'Harcourt	8	0	0	Mr. Gibbins (⅓ Gov. Grant)..	16	7	1
Oxford University	6	0	0	Joseph Keedle	5	15	0
Sir A. de Rothschild	5	0	0	M. A. Tompkins	15	0	0
D. Evans, Esq., sen.	5	0	0	Mr. Gibbins' Salary........	51	0	0
F. Calvert, Esq.	3	0	0	Ditto share of pence......	16	15	2
Lady Cooper	3	0	0	Bills (Hobday's, Chamber's,			
Rev. E. W. F. Latimer......	2	0	0	Dodwell's, Howe's, Saunder's, &c.)	6	4	4¼
Rev. T. J. Williams	1	10	0	Fuel, &c.	4	8	7
Rev. O. Symons	1	0	0	Insurance	0	15	0
Cranwell Estate	1	0	0	C. Walker's Bill	5	6	1
Mr. Belgrove	1	0	0	J. Cripps, ditto	1	9	4
Fettos Charity	1	0	0	School Cleaning	1	5	0
Messrs. Gurney	0	10	0				
Government Grant	32	14	4				
School pence	20	15	10				
Xmas tree	9	1	4				
Balance due to Treasurer	1	9	5½				
	£127	0	11½		£127	0	11½

THOS. J. WILLIAMS.
THOS. G. GOSS.
GEO. BELGROVE.

5. Waddesdon Rectory. Reproduced is the relevant page from the Waddesdon Parish Magazine for April 1870 (Rectory House Warming). As a matter of additional interest the upper paragraph of Vestry records refers to "Charity ground at Wescott" and later the "Alms Cow". The charity ground is a 13 acre field off the Bicester Road, the endowment of Lewis Fetto in 1724, and the proceeds are still used for the "apprenticing and schooling" of youngsters in the parish. "The Alms Cow" was from an unknown origin, and this charity required two cows to be kept in milk for the benefit of the poor in the village. In the early 1860s "Bunter Cows", as they were called, were kept by William Stevens, the "Waddesdon Giant", who was the tenant farmer at Lodge Hill (see photograph no. 155). In 1865 the last "Bunter cow" died, the carcase was sold for the sum of £4 and from this time the charity came to an end.

6. The builder's yard of Mr. Joseph Holland situated just to the right of the entrance to Queen Street. These premises were to be re-established in the High Street opposite the Five Arrows, next to the Gables. Mr. Holland, standing at the centre of this picture, was one of the many local builders and businessmen who prospered from the massive increase in building both on the estate and in the village. This yard was soon to be demolished to make way for the new estate offices and farm buildings.

7. A small-holder's cottage in Queen Street. Although brick built this cottage is typical of the living conditions in Waddesdon for much of the 19th century. Note the two bee "skips" in the foreground. A labourer's weekly wage was 15 to 17 shillings (75 to 85p) and the expenditure for a typical family was: bread 11 shillings and 9 pence, flour 1 shilling and 6 pence, tea 4 and a half pence, firing 1 shilling, rent 1 shilling, and other essentials 1 shilling and a penny halfpenny, no potatoes, butter or meat (as reported in the findings of the Commission on the conditions of the labouring classes in rural areas). This cottage was soon to be demolished to make way for the plantations and grounds of Waddesdon Manor, and the occupants were to be rehoused in the new village emerging a few hundred yards away.

8. The ancient Manor House of the Church (Third Portion), Atte Green or At the Green. The living at Waddesdon Church was for centuries divided into three portions, each with its own Manor House and land. The Manor of the first portion was Benthams, situated at the present old Rectory near the church, the Manor of the second portion was situated about 250 yards south-west of the church and was known as Motons, and the Manor of the third portion was located about 500 yards south-east of the church at the centre of the 1960s development known as Chestnut Close. In 1881 the three portions of the living were amalgamated and Waddesdon was reduced from sometimes having three rectors to having a single rector and one curate. They and their families were accommodated in the large rectory which had been newly constructed at Benthams. The Goss family lived at the Green for at least all the 60 years of the 20th century before the old Manor House was demolished and the land sold by the Church Commissioners. Mr. Arthur (Pete) Goss, shown in the picture, was the last tenant, during which time he served as a parish councillor for more than 50 years.

9. Bicester Hill looking remarkably as it is today except for some minor alterations to the terrace of houses, carried out after they were purchased by Miss Alice de Rothschild in the early 1900s. Originally constructed by a Mr. Bernard who had his builder's yard at the rear, they formed part of the northern extremities of the village. The cast-iron "mile-stone" at the centre of this view still exists but the orchard behind it has since grown out of all recognition and is now a thicket with only the odd pear and damson tree to betray its earlier use.

10.   The old Marlborough Arms, Waddesdon's most important inn, formed part of the manorial estates. It had been a coach stop on the Aylesbury to Bicester turnpike road, also the venue for a regular magistrates' court, and was the original village post office. After 1875 it was renamed The Five Arrows and in 1887 was demolished and gave way to the hotel which now stands in its place. Mr. Henry Turnham, the landlord, is seated on the wagonette which carried eight passengers and was used for hire work.

11.   Mr. Philip Dodwell's shop situated near the junction of High Street and Silk Street alongside the National School. Mr. Dodwell wearing the bowler hat, and Mrs. Dodwell in the shop doorway. This typical thriving village store and post office, including telegraph facilities for telegrams, was demolished around 1885 to make way for a plantation. The business was re-established in new modern premises, as can be seen in picture no. 123.

12.   The Masons Arms stood in Chapel Lane near the rear of the National School. The railings on the right mark the extremities of the playground. Over the doorway a board proclaims Thomas Holland to be the landlord, but judging by this photograph, not for much longer. Sometimes referred to as the Bricklayers Arms, this inn was shortly to be demolished, as the Baron purchased all the small plots in this part of the village to establish the periphery of the Estate grounds.

13.   This cottage stood in Crooks Yard off Queen Street; it was occupied by Levi Saunders the shoemaker, hence the board over the doorway. A typical cottage for the rural poor in this area and known locally as a "Dirt House". The walls were built by using wattle and daub methods, which consisted of willow hurdles plastered with mud and finally colour washed. The thatched roof rested directly on top of the walls and the ground floor was of bricks laid upon compressed earth. These cottages were damp and cold, with no toilet facilities. The family lavatory was in the garden with a primitive hut for privacy. The occupants subsisted on a very poor diet and in these conditions were continuously at risk from disease and fevers which were endemic in Waddesdon (see caption 14). The rent, payable to the Duke of Marlborough's agent, for this cottage standing on its plot of 16 poles (387 square metres) was £2.10s.0d. (£2.50) per year.

WADDESDON, WESCOTT,
AND OVER-WINCHENDON
PARISH MAGAZINE.

Vol. I., No. 4.]   APRIL, 1870.   [Price Twopence.

Waddesdon.

March 6th. Communicants, 40. Alms, 12s. 3d.
The Easter Communicants' Meeting will be at the School Room, on Saturday evening, April 16th, at 7.30 p.m.

PARISH REGISTER.
BAPTISMS.

Feb. 27th, Arthur, son of Thomas and Matilda Biswell.
— — Emma, daughter of John and Eliza Goss.
March 4th (private), Abel and Job, twin sons of Charles and Ann Copcutt.
— 22nd (private), James, son of James and Alice Southam.
— 24th (private), Thomas, son of Joseph and Jane Manders.
— 27th, Alfred Scutchings.

MARRIAGE.

Feb. 28th, James Saunders to Mary Ann Saunders.

BURIALS.

"He shall gather the lambs with His arm, and carry them in His bosom."

March 2nd, John Pitkin, 7 years.	March 19th, Louisa E. Southam, 4 years.
— 7th, Abel Copcutt, } 2 days.	— 24th, Eli James Fowler, 1
— 7th, Job Copcutt, }	— 24th, James Southam, 1
— 10th, Wm. Hy. Price, 5 mths.	— 25th, Thomas Manders, 7 months.
— 10th, Matilda Thorp, 2 years.	— 28th, William Hinds, — years.

The Services in the Parish Church during Holy Week will be:—Monday, Tuesday, Thursday and Saturday, at 9.0 a.m., and 7.0 p.m. Wednesday and Good Friday, at 10.30 a.m., and 7.0 p.m. Sermons each evening. The Daily Services will be continued throughout the year.

SUBSCRIPTIONS TO THE ORGAN.

	£	s.	d.
Proceeds of Tea and Collection in Church, July 31st, 1868	18	16	3
Collected by Mr. J. Thompson	2	6	2½
— by W. Keedle (London)	0	16	0
R. Rose, Esq.	4	0	0
Duke of Marlborough, K.G., £5 for 3 years	15	0	0
Rev. T. J. Williams, £4 — 3 —	12	0	0
Comte d'Harcourt, £5 — 2 —	10	0	0
David Evans, Esq.	1	0	0
Rev. Dr. Symons, Oxford	1	0	0

There will be a Concert and Tea on the Wednesday in Easter Week, in aid of the Organ.

DE FRAINE, PRINTER, WALTON-STREET, AYLESBURY.

14. During the middle years of the nineteenth century children were at mortal risk from the day they were born; none more so than the children of Waddesdon. This reproduction of the front page of the April 1870 Parish Magazine records the burial of 10 children in the month of March. The youngest died from "natural causes", but five were victims of a Scarlet Fever epidemic which had raged in the village since January, claiming 14 in all, ranging in age from 22 months to 19 years.

15.   The High Street at the Green where Silk Street emerged. The Marlborough Arms (Five Arrows) is on the right, whilst to the left are the gardens of the terraced houses which were eventually demolished to make way for The Roses. The house on the right beyond the inn was the police station.

16.   The original steam-powered flour mill of Mr. J. Taylor was established around 1850 alongside the large pond which stretched from Silk Street to Back Road. The mill's engine required a regular supply of water, and at that time the most reliable source in the village emanated from Spring Hill. The spring water was directed through the mill pond before making its way as the Wottesbroke down to Warmstone, then crossing the fields to join the River Thame at Notley Abbey near Long Crendon. Although local wheat flour was milled here, the main product was animal feed derived from imported grain. Mr. Taylor would often agree special arrangements with village small-holders and allotment tenants, undertaking to mill their corn in exchange for some cash and part of the produce. As can be seen from photograph no. 1, the mill chimney was a landmark easily visible from Lodge Hill. In 1893 a new mill was built at the lower end of Quainton Road, the machinery transferred and the old mill was demolished, thus removing an inappropriate feature from the scene as viewed from the Manor. The Taylor family, strongly associated with milling for many miles around, continued to operate the mill at Waddesdon until the 1960s. Steam power had long given way to diesel when Mr. Alfred Taylor eventually closed down operations on Waddesdon's last tangible link with the old life of self-sufficiency.

17.   A farmhouse which stood near the present day site of the Bowling Green. As befitted a farmer, the house was more substantial than most, but was destined to be demolished making way for estate parkland.

18.   Situated just off Silk Street these thatched cottages were occupied by Sarah Fowler, and Sally and Henry Taylor in 1874. As with other dwellings in this part of the village the occupants were rehoused, usually in new homes. Demolition and landscaping of the area followed apace.

19.   Not far from the present day Princes Lodge in Silk Street, this farmhouse was last lived in by Mr. Obadiah King. The farm and buildings were acquired by Baron de Rothschild *circa* 1878 and were absorbed into the new estate grounds. Plantations were being established where for centuries farm animals had been husbanded.

20.   This reverse view of photograph no. 15 shows Waddesdon High Street circa 1880. On the left are the Arthur Goodwin Alms Houses and to the right of centre the old Police Station. Beyond that The Five Arrows Inn (previously The Marlborough Arms), and on the right can be seen Dodwells' shop. This view of the High Street would completely change in the next few years, with only the Alms Houses remaining recognisable to the present day. *Note*: Just visible on Lodge Hill is the emerging new Mansion and newly planted trees in the surrounding grounds. The stand-pipe in front of the Alms Houses shows that Waddesdon is already enjoying the benefits of clean "tap water".

21. Arthur Goodwin was the Member of Parliament for Aylesbury in 1625 and 1626, and later became Lord Lieutenant of Buckinghamshire. He succeeded his father Sir Francis Goodwin as Lord of the Manor in 1634, the estate at that time encompassing nearly all the old Waddesdon Manor lands. From the outset of the civil rebellion against the Crown, his sympathies lay with the Parliamentary side. John Hampden, a leader of the rebellion and one of the protesters against the "ship tax", was a close friend. In a codicil to his will dated 1645, Arthur Goodwin instructed his executors to construct Alms Houses for the benefit of four poor widows from Waddesdon, and two from Winchendon. These Alms Houses were completed in 1657. The tenants were also given 2 shillings per week for fifty weeks each year. In 1726 the Duke of Marlborough paid for repairs to the houses and they were rebuilt in 1894 by Baron de Rothschild. (Copy of the painting of Arthur Goodwin M.P., by Van Dyck, from the Devonshire Collection. Reproduced and published by kind permission of the Chatsworth Settlement Trustees ©.)

22.   Lane End Castle, the farm-house at Eythrope Park Farm, was constructed *circa* 1752 by Sir William Stanhope, probably using materials salvaged from the demolished Eythrope House. The Rose family held the tenancy of this important portion of the estate for many generations until the 1990s. The photograph dates from circa 1900 when Mr. John Rose was the tenant. In the violent storm of 1916 the building partially collapsed. As a result the remaining battlements were removed and a pitched roof constructed, giving the building the conventional appearance which survives today (1995).

23.   A farm-house in Quainton Road which still survives as a private house (Farthings). Situated opposite the junction with New Street this house originally housed successive smallholders who farmed the surrounding fields. As recently as 1910 the dairy was still in use for the sale of fresh milk.

CHARITIES IN WADDESDON

As the 17th and 18th centuries saw a steady decline in the living conditions for the rural poor, so that period also witnessed the establishment of numerous charities aimed at providing some relief for the worst off.

Several minor "Bread Charities" which no longer exist are recorded in church accounts books, and were established upon the instructions of kindly persons who endowed sums of money or property, the proceeds of which were to be used for the purchase of bread for the poor of the village.

Although not exactly an act of charity, in 1727 a workhouse was erected, not far from the church, just down Bicester Hill. Up to 30 of the poorest people in the parish were accommodated there in very spartan living conditions and under a harsh system which was intended to give potential inmates the greatest incentive to keep out. The residents were given work to help to defray the cost to the parish, men were employed on picking stones from the fields and catching vermin, such as hedgehogs, foxes, and polecats, whilst women and children were expected to learn straw plaiting. The children were also given a rudimentary education and as they grew older were found positions or apprenticed with local farmers or tradesmen.

The very first workhouse master was William Twyman who was paid the sum of £150 per year for his labours. It functioned as intended, apart from troubles due to the poor conditions, until the late 19th century. The building still stands today but has been converted to a private residence. In 1827 there was disorder in the workhouse due to increased poverty caused by higher food prices and low wages. The poor blamed the introduction of new agricultural machinery and farming methods for their plight. In 1830 "The Machine Riots" began. These riots mostly led to the destruction of property. Farmer Mr. Ballard of Upper Winchendon had property including a new thrashing machine destroyed by fire, as did Mr. Roads, Mr. Biggs and Mr. Hirons. On the night of the 26th November in that year some 30 men went to Blackgrove Farm and after demanding that all the machinery be piled up, they fetched straw from the rick-yard and set it ablaze.

In the following year an attempt was made to "remedy" the problem by emigrating a number of families to America. Some houses belonging to the parish were sold to help with the cost, along with a grant of £50 from charity. On April 12th 1832 Mr. Benjamin Crook, the local carrier, took the 39 villagers to Aylesbury, from where they continued their journey to Liverpool by canal. This journey would have lasted about 10 days in a horse-drawn narrow boat, with little or no sanitary and sleeping facilities. For these people, who had probably never been much further afield than Aylesbury, it would have been a dreadful journey.

On the death of Arthur Goodwin the Upper Winchendon Manor and estates passed through his daughter Jane, to her husband Philip, Lord Wharton and on his death funds were left to provide bibles and prayer books for poor children who had to learn certain psalms and the Church Catechism.

Lewis Fetto, who was a resident of the hamlet of Wormstone, left in his will (dated 11th June 1724) the sum of £140 to be invested, the proceeds of which were to be used, as stated in the original accounts book which is in the County Archives, "for the Putting to school poor children to read and write", and "Putting out as apprentices such poor children of the Towne of Waddesdon". An example of this was on March 4th 1743 when the sum of £5 was paid to Mrs. Abbett for taking Henry Lee as an apprentice, and on April 23rd 1764 the sum of £4 was paid for the apprenticeship of a young girl, Ann Giner. These apprenticeships were usually for the period of seven years. The original £140 was invested in the purchase of a field situated near Westcott and it is still known as "Charity Ground".

John Beck, who lived in Bicester, left £30 for the purchase of a one acre field on the Waddesdon to Pitchcott road, also for the provision of apprenticeships.

In 1814 the Fetto and Beck Charities amalgamated and under prudent supervision provided a good charitable body in the troubled years to follow. In the year 1832 the charity granted the payment of £50 towards the cost of passages for 39 villagers, who, on the following day, 12th April, started their long journey to a new life in America. The original benefactors would have been gratified to know that the charities, 250 years after their deaths, are still helping people of the village.

William Turner and his mother arrived in the village as vagrants, and having no money they were taken in by the Rector. It soon became apparent that William was a victim of the often fatal disease smallpox. However, he recovered, although the infection he brought with him had spread through the village.

After recovering, William and his mother moved on and in adult life he became a successful trader in butter and cheese. On his death in 1784 he left the substantial sum of £3,265.11s.6d. (£3,265.57½p) to be managed in trust. The annual dividends from the investment amounted to about £80, which was distributed to the poor in the form of money, food, or clothing. By the mid-19th century about 800 persons had benefited from the trust, with payments ranging from one shilling (5p) to 10 shillings (50p) according to the number of dependants. With an average wage of between 6 to 8 shilling (30p to 40p) per week, it can be seen that an extra few shillings made an enormous difference. The capital is today invested in Unit Trusts with revised criteria for entitlement.

A COUNTRY HOME FOR THE BARON

In his quest to acquire a grand house in the country, Baron Ferdinand de Rothschild had concluded by 1874 that suitable properties were few and far between and the most likely solution may be to create his own country seat.

The Baron was first attracted to the possibilities at Waddesdon whilst hunting at Wotton with the Duke of Buckingham and Chandos. The executors of the late Duke of Marlborough were seeking to dispose of the Waddesdon and Winchendon estate and several factors recommended it for the Baron's purpose. Amongst these were a commanding view from Lodge Hill, the newly opened tramway link to the main line, access to London, and reasonable proximity to other members of the Rothschild family who had settled in the area.

On 7 July 1874 the estates, consisting of 2,763 acres, 3 roods and 37 poles with rents valued at £5,723.9s.4½d. (£5,723.47) per annum, were put up for sale at the Auction Mart, Tokenhouse Yard in London.

Many of the principal tenants attended the auction, but the property was "bought in" at £174,000 when it was clear the reserve would not be attained. The tenants' uncertainty as to the identity of their future landlord was settled when the *Bucks Herald* of August 22 1874 reported that Baron Ferdinand de Rothschild had purchased the estate for "about £200,000."

A French architect, Gabriel-Hippolyte Destailleur, was appointed to design the house and a French landscape artist, M. Laine, was entrusted with the grounds, whilst a local architect, Mr. W. Taylor of Bierton, was responsible for the new farms and cottages. Work commenced immediately and the *Bucks Herald* of 23 September reported that about 100 workers employed by the Baron had been entertained to dinner, when "a hot meal and a pleasant and jovial evening was enjoyed by all". This was perhaps the first publicised example of the enlightened attitude which was to be the hallmark of the Baron's relationship with his employees.

Meanwhile Mr. Treadwell, a well-known sheep-breeder, at his summer sale at Model Farm, Upper Winchendon, was pleased to announce that he would be continuing his business as a tenant of the new owner Baron Ferdinand de Rothschild. The Baron not only treated his employees fairly but also informed all those concerned of the plans and progress made. The scale of the enterprise and the potential prospects for the local population were enormous.

Down in the village, by the end of 1875 the larger privately owned farms of John Butterfield and Oxford University had been absorbed into the estate, along with numerous small closes, cottages and houses in Queen Street. The "tidying up" of the boundaries of the estate would continue for the next 20 years or so, with the many previous owners moving to the new model village emerging a few hundred yards to the east. Only in rare cases were the old properties retained, to be renovated and given the Rothschild crest of the Five Arrows.

The Baron was never slow to grasp a new development. For example, in 1875 he arranged the installation of the Chiltern Hills water supply to Waddesdon, Eythrope and Westcott. Although this was primarily for the Baron's purposes, he arranged for stand-pipes to be erected so that the villagers could help themselves to the first unpolluted water that many had ever tasted.

Construction of the Manor was progressing apace, and the quality of the architecture and grounds was plain for all to see. Behind all this were the many craftsmen, gardeners and others who by their skills were making the whole thing possible. The Baron's country seat was taking shape and "Black Waddesdon" was to become just a memory.

BUCKS.

Particulars and Conditions of Sale

OF A VERY IMPORTANT

FREEHOLD

MANORIAL ESTATE,

PRINCIPALLY TITHE FREE AND LAND TAX REDEEMED,

Situate about Five Miles and a Half from AYLESBURY, only One Mile from the QUAINTON STATION of the Aylesbury and Buckingham Railway, and Twelve from BUCKINGHAM;

COMPRISING THE

MANOR OF OVER WINCHENDON, the MANOR OR LORDSHIP OF WADDESDON and also the MANOR OF WESTCOTT,

WITH THEIR RIGHTS, MEMBERS, AND APPURTENANCES THERETO BELONGING;

SEVERAL FARMS,

KNOWN AS

MAINS HILL, LINCE, UPPER WINCHENDON, DECOY, WINDMILL HILL, COMP LEYS, WESTCOTT FIELD, LODGE HILL, and WESTCOTT,

WITH

SUPERIOR FARM RESIDENCES,

AND VERY

EXTENSIVE AND APPROPRIATE FARM BUILDINGS,

The "CROOKED BILLET" Public House, situate at HAM GREEN; and the "MARLBOROUGH ARMS," in the Village of WADDESDON; about

FIFTY COTTAGES,

AND

SUNDRY ENCLOSURES OF ACCOMMODATION LAND,

THE WHOLE WITHIN A RING FENCE,

Except as to a small part, in and near the Villages of WADDESDON and WESTCOTT, in one of the finest Dairy Districts in the County.

THE WHOLE EMBRACES AN AREA OF ABOUT

TWO THOUSAND SEVEN HUNDRED & SIXTY-TWO ACRES

And producing, independent of the Valuable Woods in hand, a present inadequate Rental of nearly

£5800. PER ANNUM.

Which will be Sold by Auction,

BY MESSRS.

FAREBROTHER, CLARK & CO.

At the AUCTION MART, Tokenhouse Yard, Lothbury, E.C.

On TUESDAY, the 7th day of JULY, 1874,

AT ONE FOR TWO O'CLOCK.

Particulars and Plans may be had of Messrs. WHATELEY, MILWARD & Co., Solicitors, Birmingham; and at the Offices of Messrs. FAREBROTHER, CLARK & CO., 5, Lancaster Place, Strand, London, W.C.

DRYDEN PRESS. DAVY AND SONS, 137, LONG ACRE.

24.   The front page of the extensive sale catalogue issued for the public auction on 7 July 1874. In the event the reserve price was not attained and the property was "bought in" at £174,000.

UPPER WINCHENDON.

SALE OF THE DUKE OF MARLBOROUGH'S ESTATE· —The fine manorial estate, situate in the parishes of Waddesdon, Upper Winchendon, and Cuddington, and the hamlet of Westcott, the property of the Duke of Marlborough, has been disposed of by private contract to Baron Ferdinand de Rothschild, of Leighton Buzzard. This estate, it will be remembered, was offered for sale by public auction by Messrs. Farebrother, Clark, and Co., on the 7th July last, and was then bought in at £174,000, the reserve not being reached. The price at which it has now been sold is, we understand, about £200,000. The property comprises an area of 2,763a. 3r. 37p., and produces a rental of £5,723:9:4½. Amongst the principal tenants on the estate are Mr. J. Treadwell, Mr. T. Bliss, Mr. W. Cooper, Mr. J. Bulford, Mr. W. Mead, Mr. T. Matthews, &c. Baron Ferdinand is son of Baron Anselm de Rothschild, of Vienna, whose death we recently announced.

25.   The Baron moved fast, for within a month the *Bucks Herald* published this report of the transaction.

THE DUKE OF MARLBOROUGH'S ESTATE.

Our readers are all aware by this time that the large estate in our parishes has passed out of the hands of the noble Duke to whose family it has belonged for several generations, into those of a family of foreign extraction, and of world-wide fame.   Many of us would have been content, had it so happened, to have seen no changes in our day. but as it was to be, we are well satisfied to know that the present owner, Baron Ferdinand de Rothschild, of whom personally we hear so much that redounds to his credit, and shows him to be a high-principled and large-hearted man, belongs to a family who have already proved themselves to be good landlords, and most benevolent friends to the poor and suffering, using their great wealth for the advancement of those dwelling around them.   A large house in our midst, inhabited by a very wealthy and benevolent family, will, we are sure, be to the advantage of our parish and people.   T. J. W.

THE Rev. R. B. Burges, our old and faithful minister, has spent a few days here.   He must have been gratified to see so large a congregation when he kindly preached in our Church on the evening of August 23rd.   The collection towards the Church expenses, £3 5s 8½d. was hardly worthy of so large a gathering. May his words on this occasion be long remembered by his hearers.

26.   The September 1874 edition of the Waddesdon Parish Magazine carried this rather unexciting comment on the news of the estate sale. It is evident that the Rev. Williams was already aware of the Baron's intentions to build a large house nearby.

27.   Baron Ferdinand de Rothschild was born in 1839 and died in 1898. He was a great-grandson of Mayer Amschel Rothschild, the founder of the banking house, who had sent four of his five sons to the important centres in Europe, where they established branches of the dynasty. (The five sons are represented by the five arrows of the Rothschild crest to be seen on all the estate property in Waddesdon.) Although Baron Ferdinand was born and raised in Germany and Austria, he had a preference for England, perhaps influenced by his English mother. In 1865 he married Evelina, the daughter of Baron Lionel de Rothschild of the English branch of the family. After only one and a half years of married life the Baron suffered a double tragedy when Evelina died whilst giving birth, and the child was stillborn. As a memorial to his wife the Baron endowed the Evelina Hospital for Children in Southwark. This hospital in a poor part of London was fitted out with a hundred beds and up-to-date facilities for the treatment of the sick. Its existence epitomised important aspects of the Baron's life, his benevolence and his use of progressive technology. During his lifetime the Baron became a prominent national figure, with an important circle of friends from society, politics and the arts. Many famous guests came to the Manor to sample the Baron's hospitality, and as a result the reputation of the Estate and Grounds was enhanced. From 1885 until his death in 1898, the Baron was to become known as the Liberal Member of Parliament for Aylesbury. However, his lasting reputation is to be his interest in fine art and most of all in his magnificent collection which is displayed at Waddesdon Manor. To the local population at all levels, the Baron's 25 years at Waddesdon were remembered as a time of welcomed transformation. He was known as a fair man with whom to deal and a benevolent supporter of local causes. He was the man who had put regular work and colour into many people's lives, and they were grateful, because they had known the alternative.

28.   A remarkable view of Lodge Hill shortly after the commencement of work, preparing the foundations for the Manor and surroundings gardens. This is a carefully posed photograph, each worker "frozen" at his task, mostly facing the camera and holding the pose for the duration of the quite long exposure. The gentleman in the top hat at the front centre was the foreman of the works, Mr. Judd, who subsequently settled in the village. Prior to these works commencing, Lodge Hill would have appeared much the same as other local hills, nearly bare of trees and with a farm at or near the top. The springs on the hill and the protection afforded by the elevation had been fundamental elements for human settlement here since Neolithic times.

29.   More excavations for the construction work on Lodge Hill, probably 1875. Already tree planting had commenced in the planned and selective manner which was necessary to achieve the aims of the Baron.

30.   Landscaping activities under way, *circa* 1875, to provide the secluded effect for the south driveway at the point where Lodge Hill adjoins Westcott Hill. This view was soon to become almost unrecognisable with the planting of many varieties of fir trees.

31.   The Manor under construction 1878. Once again a specially posed photograph from which so much can be observed. At the right and left foreground can be seen the rails of the tramway which enabled delivery of the heavy building materials from the Westcott side of the hill. A spur from the Wotton tramway was extended from Westcott to the foot of the hill then up the hill and into the building site. The trucks being unhitched from the locomotive and hauled up the slope by a steam winch. A steam crane is operating at the right of the picture and the arms for several other hoists can be seen on the upper levels of the construction. The foundation stone was laid in August 1877 when 400 workmen dined at a celebration dinner, whilst children of Waddesdon and Winchendon enjoyed a "treat" in the grounds.

32.   The steam locomotive (Aveling and Porter) and rolling stock used on the Wotton tramway, *circa* 1878. At this time two of these locomotives were employed on the tramway which was utilised to transport the immense quantities of building materials, including stone from Bath, used in the construction of the Manor. (© London Transport Museum.)

33.   Stonemasonry one of the many specialist trades which were imported to carry out the building work for the Manor, was carried out on-site as can be seen from this photograph of 1877.

34. The Manor soon after its completion. This view of the south front clearly shows the newly established flower beds and immature trees.

35. Visitors enjoying the view at the south front of the Manor, *circa* 1900.

36.   The north front of the Manor with the main entrance door at the centre of the photograph, *circa* 1890.

37.   A view of the north front taken on the occasion of a visit by the Prince of Wales, later to become King Edward VII. Carriages are lined up near the entrance whilst on the near lawn can be discerned the line markings of a tennis court and behind that a small marquee where refreshing drinks could be dispensed, *circa* 1890.

38.   Queen Victoria leaving Waddesdon Manor at the Grand Lodge, Waddesdon cross-roads. One of the prints widely used at
the time by national and local press. On Wednesday May 14th 1890 Queen Victoria bestowed upon the Baron the
comparatively rare compliment of a private visit. No doubt having heard from the Prince of Wales, who was a regular visitor, of
the modern marvels and wonders at Waddesdon, she had let it be known that an invitation for a royal visit would be in order.
The visit excited a tremendous local response, with the route from Aylesbury Station decorated with bunting and patriotic
banners, whilst crowds from far and wide gathered at vantage points to see and greet their legendary monarch. The national
press recorded the day's events in long double page articles which also described the perfection of the Manor grounds, and
illustrated the commemorative tree planting and departure with the aid of prints. *Note*: at this time film and cameras demanded
long exposure times, and therefore could not be used for moving objects, nor was it yet possible to reproduce photographs in
newspapers, hence the use of prints.

39.   The south side of the Manor from the neighbouring slope showing how the trees had become established, *circa* 1896. Already the south drive is hidden and the landscaping is beginning to take on the completed appearance which M. Laine and the Baron had visualised in 1875. Five photographs, *circa* 1902 and numbered 40 to 44, are included solely to offer readers an appreciation of the magnificent style and mature perfection which the Baron had achieved inside the Manor. Although the building had incorporated a unique blend of traditional architecture and modern innovations, the room interiors were created from art and craftsmanship of mainly pre-revolutionary France. The story of this accomplishment forms part of Mrs. James de Rothschild's book, *The Rothschilds at Waddesdon Manor*, first published in 1979.

40.   The Red Drawing Room.

41. The Smoking Room.

42. The Grey Drawing Room.

43. The Picture Gallery.

44. The French Gallery.

45. A group of workers temporarily distracted from labours at the stables, *circa* 1900. As can be seen from this photograph, there are several stable-hands and rather more painters, just an indication of the number of jobs provided by the presence of the big house. In 1900 there were 17 carriages of various types which were maintained and staffed at the stables by 14 men in summer and 13 in winter.

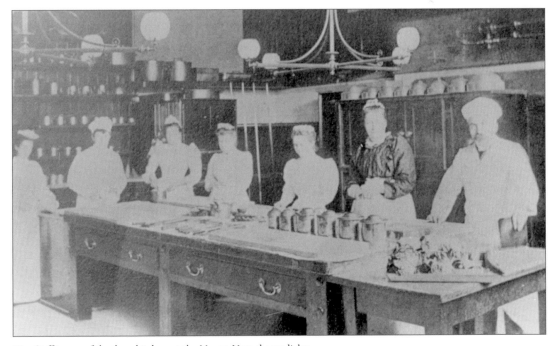

46. Staff in one of the three kitchens at the Manor. Note the gas lights.

47.   The gas house at Westcott was at the junction of Westcott Field Farm road and the Ashendon to Westcott Road. It was built in 1883 to supply gas to the Rothschild estate at Waddesdon Manor. Coal was brought to Quainton by rail, transferred to the Wotton tramway where it was then carried to a siding at Westcott which had previously been used for the transporting of building materials for the Manor. Gas was then manufactured and piped up the hill to the Manor, stables, and laundry. The by-products such as tar and ammonia were returned by rail via Quainton to Silvertown in London. The gas house manager was Mr. Albert Evans, who in 1881 joined his uncle Mr. J. Evans at Mr. Lionel de Rothschild's Ascott House, Wing, where he was taught the art of gas making. He spent two years at Wing before taking charge at Westcott in 1883. When the First World War came in 1914, coal became increasingly difficult to obtain, and so the gasworks closed in 1916. Mr. Evans then worked for a time at the Quainton Road gasworks in Waddesdon, from where he retired.

48.   The magnificent gates at the Grand Lodge, Waddesdon cross-roads. Employees of Mr. J. Read, one of numerous local builders who supplemented the maintenance craftsman retained by the estate, renovating the paintwork and gilding on the gates. These aspects of the decorator's trade would have been otherwise unheard-of in a rural village. Photograph *circa* 1905.

49.   Silk Street and the annual visit of Mr. W. Stevens and his steam-roller, *circa* 1910. Seated at the front is Mr. Bert Jones. Each year the driveways were rolled and raked to maintain the immaculate appearance necessary to match the very smart verges and fences. In the background is Webbs, the draper's shop.

50.   An interesting view of the stables, possible only because the trees had not yet reached maturity, *circa* 1910.

51.   Built in 1884, the stables provided accommodation for all the carriages, horses grooms and stable hands required to operate the transport facilities for the Manor. Once again the Baron had displayed his enlightened attitude in enlisting the help of his stud groom and the builder, as well as the architectural designer Gabriel-Hippolyte Destailleur, in planning the layout and elevation of the stables.

52.   The aviary in all its splendour, and with parrots perched at intervals in the open. Although this photograph was taken around 1905, the aviary and nearby deer pens had been established more than 15 years.

53.   The entrance gates and the Reading Room in Waddesdon High Street, *circa* 1908. The Reading Room was amongst the first of the Baron's philanthropic provisions for the village, a library and club for all the male workers in the community, where non-alcoholic refreshments and warm, comfortable accommodation were available for reading and the enjoyment of indoor games.

54.   The pony-drawn mower at the Cricket Field with the splendid Pavilion in the background, *circa* 1910. Miss Alice de Rothschild was a generous patron of the village sports clubs, particularly ensuring that the cricket field, the pavilion, and tea rooms adjacent were maintained in perfect condition. Full-time staff were employed during the summer and Waddesdon Cricket Club enjoyed facilities second to none in the area. Note the leather boots on the pony's hoofs to minimise damage to the playing surface. Holding the pony's bridle is George Carter.

55.   The Grand Lodge at Waddesdon cross-roads, *circa* 1910. This lodge entrance to the estate grounds offered advantages over the main entrance in Waddesdon High Street, not least the privacy, convenience and gentler slopes leading right up to the Manor. Just about a mile away on the road to Pitchcott was the Aylesbury and Buckingham Railway line, and this point was chosen by the Baron for the site of Waddesdon Manor Station. This station was opened on January 1st 1897, making the Grand Lodge entrance more appropriate for the arrival and departure of the Baron and his celebrated guests.

56.   A very early view of the glass-houses viewed from the slopes of Lodge Hill. To the left can be seen the young plantation of trees which were to fully clothe the hill within a few years. The nearest part of the complex was known as Top Glass and beyond that was the Fruit Range. This magnificent array of glass, together with surrounding vegetable and fruit gardens, provided the household needs of the Manor as well as beautiful arrangements of flowers and exotic plants to be enjoyed by house-guests and visitors alike. In the tallest houses were palms and within the others were peaches, figs, grapes, nectarines, cherries, and numerous traditional fruits. The pathways were of gravel and bordered by immaculate flower beds and hedges. Many commentators believed Waddesdon to have the largest area under glass of any private house in the country.

57.   The gardens at the Manor in the North Front lawns illustrate the craftsmanship and artistic design in the flower beds, manicured lawns and surrounding shrubbery. This photograph was taken from the Rockery Road, *circa* 1910. Throughout the grounds there were many similar features requiring the close attention of an army of craftsmen employed by the head gardener.

58.   This view of the fountain and rose garden was taken from Top Glass. Throughout the gardens all the pools contained goldfish, which added to the visual pleasures and proved the good state of the water, *circa* 1905.

59.   This expansive pathway was known as the Herbaceous Walk. At the far end is the Fruit Range and in the distance can be seen the poplar trees which provided a landmark at Littleton Manor Farm for many years. Photograph *circa* 1905.

60.   The Top Rose Walk taken from Top Glass, *circa* 1905. The wrought-iron gates led from the glass houses into the kitchen gardens. This picture shows how yew trees were planted to provide shelter whilst adding to the decorative effect and by now the well-established appearance of the gardens belies the fact that only a few years earlier cattle and sheep seemed destined to graze these slopes for ever.

61. To tend to the gardens a small army of men were employed, many of them from the locality. However, the need for suitable staff on or near the gardens was so great, that staff were recruited from all over the country and accommodated in the Bothy, which was built at the far end of Queen Street, opposite the head gardener's house. Here we see a group of young men attired for their day off, with perhaps a duty gardener, posing at the highly decorative gates in the snow, *circa* 1910.

62. Top Glass, main entrance to the complex, *circa* 1908, giving an established and mature appearance in complete contrast to that displayed in photograph no. 56.

63 and 64.   The staff of Waddesdon gardens, *circa* 1910. A proportion of estate staff were outsiders, some of whom married local people and settled down in the village. The remainder eventually moved to other stately homes and civic gardens, usually on promotion, as the "Waddesdon Standard" was admired everywhere. Front row, far right, in photograph 63 is Mr. Ernest Dormer, who started work at Waddesdon gardens on leaving school, and later became head gardener at Eythrope, where he worked until his death aged 68. His two sons Bill and Laurie also worked as gardeners at Waddesdon and Eythrope on leaving school. Seated in photograph 64 are, at the left, Mrs. Harry Turner, Mr. Johnson in the bowler hat (head gardener), Mr. Wicks (foreman gardener), and Mrs. Speed, Bothy housekeeper.

65. Workers admiring their handiwork in the Dairy gardens, *circa* 1910. As with all agricultural and horticultural work a certain amount of care has to be provided, even on a Sunday. Because of the size of the gardens, weekend working for some was the "norm," not voluntary, but as part of a roster. This apart the normal working week was five and a half days (55 hours).

66. A view of the rose beds from the Dutch Gardens looking towards the Fountain and Top Glass. The Dutch Gardens included an outstanding display of tulips in springtime.

67.   Estate workers and painters at Wormstone "Lakes". Second from left is Will Saunders, fourth from left Charlie Rolfe and Harry Rolfe. The "lakes", decorative ponds on each side of the road, are connected by the bridge in the picture, and fed by one of the numerous springs on Waddesdon Hill. This photograph dates from around 1910, and gives some idea of the smart appearance maintained throughout the estate.

68.   The Rose garden at the Dairy was a popular feature of the garden tour which most of the Baron's and Miss Alice's guests were invited to take. At the centre of this photograph is the Buttery, *circa* 1908.

69.   Another view of the gardens at the Dairy, *circa* 1912. The head dairyman's house is at the end of the garden. As with all the prestige gardens on the estate the maintenance was carried out by staff from "The Gardens". The pergola at the right of picture was later moved to the grounds near the Manor.

70.   The Second Range House, with its masses of blooms grown principally for house-decoration, *circa* 1910.

71.   The corridor and Palm House providing an interesting and exotic transition between the glass-houses, *circa* 1905.

72.   This is the corridor leading from the front entrance of Top Glass to the Palm House. Photograph *circa* 1905.

73.   The five photographs 73 to 77 illustrate the elaborate Water and Rock Garden which were created on the north facing side of Lodge Hill. This setting, perhaps more in keeping with a mountainous region than the Vale of Aylesbury, provided a very different opportunity for the village photographer, Mr. Albert Cherry. In photograph no. 73 he positioned his daughter Norah at the bridge over the rock pool. Photographs *circa* 1910.

74.

75.

76.

77.

78. The "Show-ring" standard exhibited by this pony and trap and smartly dressed driver is an example of the normal turnout of those employed at the Manor. This photograph was taken *circa* 1910 in the High Street, on Bicester Hill outside the gates leading to the Estate Yard and the workshops.

79.   Miss Alice de Rothschild purchased this de Dion Bouton in 1909. It was the first motor car owned by Miss Alice and it is here photographed at the stables, where it had presumably ousted the more traditional carriage and horses. This motor car was later sold to Mr. Ewart Newman, butcher and farmer, who lived at The Grove and later still it passed to Mr. David Evans, motor engineer, who modified it for hire as a licensed hackney carriage, Waddesdon's first taxi.

80.   Beachendon Farm House, *circa* 1900. Originally a 17th century farmhouse standing on a prominence near the River Thame at Eythrope, this extended and fine looking dwelling displays the hallmarks of the Rothschild's farm tenancies. Robust buildings, often exposed to the elements but comfortable and modern for their day. Beachendon Farm has a history going back beyond the Domesday Survey and has for centuries had close ties with the Eythrope Estate. Until the 1930s the farm had been in the tenancy of the Flower family for more than 100 years.

81 and 82. Waddesdon Manor Station was built especially for Baron Ferdinand de Rothschild, who had important interests in the development of the local rail system. The station, situated off the Pitchcott Road on the old Aylesbury to Buckingham Railway line, was opened in 1897. With the incorporation of this line into the national network, the Baron and his guests had ready access to the whole country, for arrangements were in place that allowed them to halt "through" trains at this station. These two photographs date from *circa* 1910. Villagers could use the scheduled services by cycling the two miles by road, or more likely by walking over public footpaths across the fields. At such a distance from the village the station in time became uneconomical and it was closed in 1936. The platforms remain to this day (1995). (© London Transport Museum.)

83 and 84.   The Pavilion at Eythrope, *circa* 1900. Eythrope lies within the Parish of Waddesdon and in ancient times the lands formed part of the manorial estate. However, the large area held by Miles Crispin at the time of the Domesday Survey was fragmented with the passing of the centuries and Eythrope became a separate estate. For many years Eythrope had its own grand house, situated not far from the artificial lake through which the redirected River Thame slowly flows. For a long period the house was uninhabited and neglected, then finally demolished in 1810. The building materials were sold off, together with the other finer examples purchased by local "well-to-do" owners. For example Ceely House, now the County Museum in Aylesbury, is said to have the porch and doorway from Eythrope House. In 1875, when Miss Alice de Rothschild bought the Eythrope estate from the d'Harcourt family, practically all traces of the previous house had disappeared. It was therefore on a bare site that Miss Alice proceeded to construct the Pavilion in 1883. The architect was Mr. George Devey, the construction was largely in brickwork and the finished house, uniquely, was designed for daytime use only. On the advice of her doctor Miss Alice decided to avoid the risk of sleeping in damp, low-lying accommodation by eliminating the temptation. She therefore travelled back and forth to Waddesdon Manor whenever she was in residence. Although a short distance from the site of the original house, the Pavilion enjoyed an excellent view of the river and surrounding park.

Eythrope.

85. Miss Alice de Rothschild at Eythrope, *circa* 1890. Waddesdon Manor and the Estate was bequeathed to Miss Alice upon the death of Baron Ferdinand in 1898. She carried on most of the traditions which had become established by her brother and initiated a few of her own, the most telling perhaps her insistence upon perfection in all things, particularly in the grounds and gardens. This requirement and its attainment became known as "The Waddesdon Standard", the benefits of which were to be seen everywhere Waddesdon staff lived and worked. Her benevolence to the local population was constant, but usually not publicised. Encouragement for self-advancement was evident in her support for education, sport, horticulture, and agriculture. Perhaps most telling were two small aspects affecting the very poorest in the community. The first was her insistence upon being kept informed of those who had a serious illness; then nourishing food would be delivered. The second was an unwritten instruction that no local man wanting work around Christmas-time was to be denied. The Great War and all the travails which came with it affected things in every way. By the early 1920s sufficient time had elapsed despite the failing health of Miss Alice for a "normality" to return. In 1922, almost 25 years after the death of her brother the Baron, Miss Alice passed away. Memories of this period for local villagers varied considerably. In the majority were those who emphasised the stability, the strong community still dependent upon the Estate, and the benefits derived. There were others who thought "the good old days" ended with the Baron; who were aggrieved that women felt compelled to curtsey whenever Miss Alice drove past, and that men working in the Estate grounds were expected to make themselves scarce whenever Miss Alice was nearby. The near certainty that these customs arose from accepted 19th century etiquette on one hand, and the over-zealous interpretation of instructions by managers on the other, was lost in the mists of time. Such is life. Miss Alice's heir to the Manor, gardens and Estate was her great-nephew, Mr. James de Rothschild.

86.   James and Dorothy de Rothschild. In 1922 the Waddesdon Manor Estate was inherited by Mr. James de Rothschild, and he and his wife Dorothy made Waddesdon their home. The following 70 years was a period of massive change everywhere, and this of course was reflected in the management and relationship of the Manor with the local community. Many fascinating details are contained in Mrs. de Rothschild's book *The Rothschilds at Waddesdon Manor*; however, the story of Waddesdon village post-1925 falls outside the main scope of this book. Suffice to say that Mr. and Mrs. James de Rothschild carried on the principles established by the Baron. Things were changing, but the affection earned by their concern and attention for the local community was maintained throughout. Upon the death of James de Rothschild in 1957, the Manor and 160 acres of surrounding grounds were bequeathed to The National Trust. This again is another story.

SECTION THREE

THE NEW VILLAGE

D uring the last quarter of the nineteenth century a great many people in the locality were affected by the development of Waddesdon Manor and the estate. Jobs, business and the resultant prosperity were not restricted to the village of Waddesdon. However, it was in this village and the surrounding hamlets that radical changes occurred in the physical aspect.

This section illustrates how the new village emerged as the Baron's plans took shape on Lodge Hill. Queen Street, Silk Street, and the High Street connecting them, lost most of their cottages, whilst Chapel Lane disappeared altogether. Plantations of trees grew where cottage gardens had hitherto flourished. New houses and shops were constructed in Quainton Road, Baker Street, and the High Street and a new road, Frederick Street, provided building land for more than 100 houses.

Taylor's Mill and Dodwell's Shop re-appeared in similar guises elsewhere in the village, whilst other notable businesses such as the Silk Mill and the Masons Arms disappeared for ever. The Baptist Chapel was replaced by a new building in Frederick Street.

Waddesdon's growing prosperity was reflected in the modern services which were provided: tap water in 1875, coal-gas and street lighting in 1883, and a sewage system in 1904. All many years in advance of most other villages in the area.

By the time of the Baron's death in 1898 much of the top end of the village, south of the High Street, had already become established Estate property, the main exception being the National School. It remained for Miss Alice to complete the remodelling of that part of the village. In due course "The Roses" and "The Cedars" were built in place of old cottages, whilst the villagers displaced by these grand homes were rehoused in New Street. A new National School was constructed off Baker Street and the original building was renovated to become "The Institute". The new village was now complete.

87.   The church viewed from the west in winter-time. This photograph, *circa* 1895, can be compared with photograph no. 2 where the differences in the structure can be clearly seen. The rebuilding of the tower and other exterior renovations required a massive fund-raising effort on the part of all those concerned. The tower alone cost £1,900 and the other work took the total amount to around £3,000. Work was started by Waddesdon builder H.H. Sherwin in June 1891 and the new tower was dedicated in June 1892. By far the most generous donor to the fund was Baron Ferdinand de Rothschild, who also attended and supported fund-raising functions held in the Manor grounds and the Reading Room.

88.   The main pathway leading from the south entrance of the church-yard showing the avenue of horse-chestnut trees that gave such a beautiful welcome to visitors. On the right is a gas lamp-standard, one of the many modern conveniences which Waddesdon enjoyed at this time. Gas lighting for street illumination was installed after the Provincial Gas and Lighting Company commenced operations at their plant down Quainton Road in 1883. The Manor had its own gas-works at Westcott by this time. Photograph *circa* 1900.

89. The south front, *circa* 1895, giving a good view of the completed renovations to the church. To the right can be seen the Rectory conveniently located at Benthams, the Manor of the First Portion.

90. A rare view of the interior of St Michael and All Angels' church taken before the installation of the rood screen.

91. Queen Street, *circa* 1908, viewed from the far end of the Estate yard buildings with the church in the background. Note the way in which the privet hedge has been trimmed to leave the wrought iron fencing protruding by the extent of the hooped top. One imagines the appreciation of the hedge clipper when he had completed his task!

92. A reverse view to photograph no. 91, *circa* 1904. The imposing house on the right provided accommodation for the head foreman of the gardens and the cottage just in Queen Street was also provided for the head horse-man working from the Estate yard.

93 and 94.   Summer and winter views along Queen Street taken from near the West Gate of the church-yard, *circa* 1905. On the left is the Bell Inn and on the right the Ship Inn. The Ship and the cottages were soon to be demolished to make way for "The Cedars".

95.   Queen Street and the Estate farm buildings photographed from the church tower, *circa* 1900. In the foreground can be seen the rear gardens and sheds belonging to the Ship Inn and the terraced cottages; also visible at the end of the gardens are lavatories and pigsties. Many of the villagers kept livestock of some kind, including pigs, rabbits, or poultry, to supplement their incomes and family diets.

96.   Almost the same view about ten years later. The Ship Inn which had belonged to the Aylesbury Brewery Company had been secured by Miss Alice de Rothschild in an exchange deal involving the Crooked Billet at Woodham. The inn and all the cottages in the vicinity had been razed to the ground to be replaced by "The Cedars". Miss Alice used this house in a "Grace and Favour" style to accommodate two friends, Miss Chinnery and Miss Gilling-Lax. Garden staff and house servants attended daily from the Manor.

97.   Bicester Hill, *circa* 1912. Heaps of road-mending stones and the absence of a footpath indicate that pedestrians normally used the unmetalled roadway along with the remainder of the "traffic". The gas lamp standard visible in the hedge remains to this day (1995). The house on the right was originally constructed as a workhouse in 1727. It was administered by the overseer of the poor, who was responsible for the maintenance and sustenance of the destitute families of the parish. The house was purchased by Miss Alice, modified and subsequently used to accommodate senior estate administrators.

98.   The new Institute shortly after its procurement by Miss Alice de Rothschild in 1910. As can be seen at the gable end nearest the camera, some modifications have been carried out externally, but the following photograph gives the reader an illustration of the finished alterations. Beyond the Institute is the Reading Room, which combined the house of the Manor gatekeeper with a library and club for working men in the village. Constructed in 1883, the Club comprised a coffee bar, reading and lecture rooms, and a library of some 200 volumes. Additionally, the Club was a meeting-place for Waddesdon's Cricket Club.

99. The Institute, *circa* 1914. The building has been given "the Rothschild treatment", and the old school-room extended by about 4ft (1.25 metres). The bell-tower now accommodates a three-faced clock, and the plaque to the Rev. Walton on the gable end of the school-house was replaced by a Five Arrows sign. The whole effect is now totally in keeping with the many prestige buildings that line the High Street at this end of the village. The Institute was a club for the senior officials on the estate and for invited tradesmen from the village and surrounding community. In many ways it was a more select model of the Reading Room.

100. The High Street looking due east from the entrance gates of the Manor grounds, *circa* 1905. The window blinds opposite at number 114 shade the high-class boots and shoes which were displayed in the shop of Mr. E. Garner. The next house in view is number 110 and was the home and part-time business premises of Mr. John Goss, who sold cooked meat and sausages. At this time the village had more than 60 businesses catering for almost all the regular needs of the population. Amongst these enterprises were six bakers, four undertakers, two barbers, a photographer, a rat-catcher, chimney sweeps, dressmakers, butchers, grocers, and of course a grave-digger. (Photograph reproduced by kind permission of the Royal Commission on the Historical Monuments of England © RCHME Crown copyright.)

101.   The High Street taken around 1900, from almost the same viewpoint as the previous photograph . On the left is Webbs' drapery and outfitters shop housed in a fine new Rothschild building. In the distance can be seen the roof of the new Village Hall, whilst the Five Arrows Hotel and the Rothschild houses at the edge of The Square or Green complete the picture.

102.   "The Roses", *circa* 1910. This imposing residence was built in 1904 on the site originally containing a row of cottages (see photograph no. 15). Miss Alice continued her development of the village by building this house especially for the village doctor. Beyond "The Roses" is another large house, "The Gables", which in this case was to be extensively renovated, given the Five Arrows crest and used to house senior estate staff. It had previously been the home and business premises of the builder, Mr. Joseph Holland.

103.   Another view of "The Roses" some years later, *circa* 1918. The trees in the garden have grown several feet taller and the brickwork has a mature look about it. Behind the railings is the young hedge which in later years was to totally obscure this house from the eyes of passers-by.

104.   From a vantage point off Silk Street the photographer has recorded the scene of 1885 looking across the High Street towards the church, and the top of the old tower is just visible above the trees. The horse-drawn wagon is emerging from Chapel Lane and the grassed area in the foreground was the site of the village pound, whilst beyond that lies The Green or the Square, as it was variously known.

105.   The reverse view to photograph no. 104 taken some 25 years later, showing Silk Street at its most impressive. The maturing horse chestnut trees in blossom, and the wide and immaculate drive (known by three names – The Carriage Drive, Silk Street, also Silver Street). The beautiful wrought-iron gates at Princes Lodge can be seen in the distance, and all signs of the old village at this point have completely disappeared.

106.   These new homes were amongst the first to be built in the distinctive "Rothschild style" in Waddesdon. Standing at the High Street, junction with Silk Street they were constructed by John Thompson and Son. The builder is pictured here at the fence, *circa* 1883. See also photograph no. 105.

107.   Near to Chapel Lane and facing Bradfords Alley these two houses (photographs nos 107 and 108) were also constructed by John Thompson and Son around 1882. This photograph also provides a glimpse of a cottage in Chapel Lane shortly to be demolished in favour of woodland.

108.   The same pair of houses, but photographed from the opposite end, shows the depressingly bare slopes of Lodge Hill in the left background, whilst next to the house at left foreground are several tree plantings, the first stages of the woodland which soon enveloped this area of old Waddesdon.

109. The Gas House at Westcott photographed from the Ashendon Road *circa* 1882. The southern slopes of Lodge Hill can be seen at right background, quite bare of trees. The builder John Thompson is once again in the picture, as was his custom with all photographs of his finished work.

110. Newly-built Rothschild houses in Silk Street opposite Princes Lodge, *circa* 1880. This rather unusual style, with few windows and splendid chimneys, became quite common in the village, although no two houses of this type were exactly alike. The original common hawthorn hedge was soon to be uprooted and a smart wrought-iron fence with privet hedge was to take its place. The lady in the porch was Mrs. Ford. In the background to the left of the house can be seen the chimney of the old steam mill.

111.   Princes Lodge in Silk Street, with the last independently owned house showing just beyond. This old house was demolished around 1903. From 1843 to 1890 a branch of the Aylesbury Silk factory was situated in Silk Street. It provided work for up to 40 women under the manager William Moscrop.

112.   The village cricket field was laid out about 300 yards behind Princes Lodge, in a field previously known as Kings Green. The Baron provided the field, the pavilion and the ground- staff. In 1907 Miss Alice added the Tea Rooms shown on the left of this photograph. A superb venue for numerous summertime activities, with the pavilion also serving as the platform for group photographs, as will be seen in the section on "Village Life".

113. The first of three different views of The Five Arrows Hotel, *circa* 1887. This photograph was taken on the completion of the building, but the signs, lamps, weather vanes, guttering and glass in the windows were not yet fitted. The gardens had not been started, and the typical Rothschild hoop-top fence was still to be erected (note workmen with spade and wheel-barrow). The building at the far left of picture is all that remained of the Marlborough Arms after the front-facing gable end section had been removed to provide an entrance to the rear of the hotel (see photograph no. 10). *Note*: stone horse-mounting step also not yet built.

114. The Five Arrows Hotel, *circa* 1890. Standing on the site of the old Marlborough Arms, this prestige hotel was completed in 1887, and the first landlord was Henry Turnham. The building was designed by W. Taylor and Son, and built of local stone and red brick with Monk's Park stone dressing in the Old English Domestic style. It consisted of concert and audit rooms, a dining room to seat 100 persons, and 10 spacious bedrooms. The stables and yard buildings are also in this style. The two weather vanes have the initials F.R. for Ferdinand de Rothschild, and the stone step at the left foreground was to assist riders in mounting their horses. Before the First World War, the Waddesdon Philharmonic Society provided musical entertainment on special occasions from the balcony.

115.   A striking view of the Five Arrows Hotel, *circa* 1900, with the club-room just beyond (left background). The wagonette was used by Mr. Turnham in one of his other business enterprises as a carrier, a regular hiring being the transportation of the village football team on away fixtures.

116.   The High Street, *circa* 1888, viewed from the blacksmith's and farrier's workshop next to the White Lion public house. At this time the proprietor of the workshop was Mr. Thomas Gilson, whose family had run this business for more than 50 years. The houses on the left were all to go to make way for woods, a new road (Baker Street) and the Village Hall. The small cottage just beyond the White Lion was demolished and replaced by a single house in 1922. Just to the left of the telegraph pole can be discerned a stand-pipe, one of several installed in the High Street, supplying the villagers with fresh water since 1876.

117. Waddesdon High Street, *circa* 1910. Despite the unmetalled road and the undefined verges, an air of quiet prosperity prevails. The White Lion is now an hotel giving visitors and travellers an alternative to the grander Five Arrows Hotel.

118. Pensioners leaving the Village Hall after distribution of Miss Alice's gifts, *circa* 1905. Baron Ferdinand built the hall in 1897 to serve as a venue for enlightening functions for the villagers. This building was designed by W. Taylor and Son, architects from Aylesbury who had been retained by the Baron for most of the building works on the estate. It is said that the two chimneys were added at the Baron's suggestion, although they are purely ornamental. The whole construction cost £3,000, surely one of the best village halls in the area.

119.   The Arthur Goodwin Almshouses, *circa* 1905. These houses were extensively renovated in 1894 by the Baron, who crowned the smart new appearance with the "Rothschild-style" chimneys clearly shown in this picture.

120.   The entrance to Baker Street, the Village Hall and the Almshouses, viewed from the north side of the High Street. This photograph of around 1900 records a totally new aspect of the village. Note the gas lamp-standard on the left and the magnificent elm trees beyond.

121.   The High Street looking east from outside the Village Hall, *circa* 1925. At the left can be seen the premises of James (Jimmy) Jones, Motor and Cycle Engineer, and next door Humphrey's grocery shop and post office. On the Green at the right, small children can be seen at play. Although the field was known as "the Green" it was in fact owned by the church, was totally enclosed and formed part of the Manor of the Third Portion (Atte Green). Fortunately, Mr. A. J. (Pete) Goss the tenant farmer was very tolerant, not objecting to youngsters of all ages using the "Green" for recreation.

122.   A fine view of the High Street looking west from the Five Arrows Hotel, *circa* 1910. Opposite is the builder's yard of Mr. J. Holland alongside "The Gables", next is "The Roses", newly completed, then Webb's shop. This view captures the idyllic atmosphere which arouses so much nostalgia in many of the older villagers.

123.   The High Street *circa* 1900, looking due east from the same spot as photograph 122. On the left is Mr. P. Dodwell's new premises. The hardwood door on the left leads into a room furnished for the Baron's personal use when he required the telegraph service. Next to the shop was the end of terrace house used by an Estate worker, but soon to become the village Police Station, then the Coffee Tavern run by Mrs. Betsy Rolfe, who previously had a Beer Shop near Warmstone, next Mr. Collyer the tailor who supplied the Manor staff with their livery, and finally the village photographer Mr. Albert Cherry, who also collected the rates and advised credit firms on the circumstances of villagers.

124.   The High Street from outside the Village Hall, *circa* 1900. The houses on the left, near to the Five Arrows Hotel, included the Police Station, which was soon to transfer across the road to the terraced house next to Dodwell's shop. The covered waggon is parked outside Crook's Egg Packing Station, known locally as "the Egglars". This waggon was driven each week to London delivering eggs and poultry including "Aylesbury Ducks". *En-route* these products were delivered to shops, whilst other similar goods were collected for sale further on. The round trip would take two whole days. Lights for street illumination were installed after the Provincial Gas and Lighting Company commenced operations at their plant in Quainton Road in 1883 (see photograph no. 150). The Manor had its own gasworks at Westcott by this time.

125.   On April 26 1908 the village awoke to find a freak snow storm had blanketed the area to a depth of about four inches. For the village photographer this was too good an opportunity to miss.

126.   Franklin's shop, *circa* 1880. One of the few businesses which was not physically altered by the reshaping of the village. This photograph is a first-class example of the care taken by the professional photographer at that time. The reader will see how everyone in the picture is posing for the camera, even the man at the flour-loft door. Both of the delivery carts were owned by Mr. Franklin and used for bread and grocery delivery services in the locality.

127.   The White Lion Hotel, *circa* 1910. The cottage just beyond the hotel was the home and shop of Kitty Allen, who sold home-made sweets and rock. The house was demolished and replaced by a new house (Southview) in 1922.

128.   Saunders' drapers, outfitters and hardware shop (Manchester House), in the High Street, *circa* 1910. As with most village shops of this period, a wide range of goods were available here, anything from a suit or dress, to a pound of nails or a gallon of paraffin. To the right can be seen two tall pipes. These were vent pipes for the sewerage system which had been installed in 1904. Known locally as "stink pipes", they became the venue for children's games, hence the scuffed surface of their bases.

129.   Frederick Street from the top of the hill with Herring's bakers and grocers shop on the right near the middle of the picture. This street came into existence as the population shifted from the vicinity of the Estate grounds into new homes elsewhere. In 1875 Mr. Frederick Mason owned a shop and land parallel to Quainton Road, and this land was the start of the street. Hence the name derived from the original owner. This photograph was taken around 1905.

130.   Another view of Frederick Street, *circa* 1900. On the extreme left is the Cart Shed which was to become Frederick Street Room, a wooden hut which was provided for hire by the church, and was used for a wide variety of meetings and entertainment. A regular use was a Monday lunch-time thrift club where villagers could pay their few coppers, to provide a sum against the purchase of coal and clothing. Cubs and Scouts, singing groups, and musical practice sessions enlivened the vicinity at night-time.

131.   Grace's Grocery Stores, *circa* 1910. As with many village stores of the day, Grace's sold just about everything in the line of provisions, including ales and stout! Miss Emma Grace and her brother John seen here on the right of the doorway somehow managed to include pork butchery and bakery in their business. The bakery was underground, with goods access through the wooden flap shown raised at the left of the doorway. At Christmas-tide Miss Alice de Rothschild issued vouchers for pork to deserving villagers, who could then claim their joint at either Grace's or Price's butchers' shop.

132.   Quainton Road, *circa* 1895. Children safely playing in the street, the boy leaning against the fence has "stilts" made from treacle tins and tied to his shoes with string. At the near left is the shop of Joey Owen selling just about everything one might need at short notice. On the right of the road, in the distance, is Mrs. Keedle's shop, also selling just about everything from sweets and tinned food to paraffin.

133. Quainton Road from the opposite direction to photograph no. 132, around 1920. The internal combustion engine is now in evidence. The houses at near left were built by Miss Alice de Rothschild for estate workers. These were the days when a tied house was considered to be an act of benevolence, and these up-to-date homes were a good "perk" of the job.

134. New Street, *circa* 1910. Several of these houses were built to house families previously living near the Ship Inn and now displaced to make way for "The Cedars".

135.   The High Street looking eastwards from the Quainton Road junction, *circa* 1900. Except for the absence of traffic, a view that is instantly recognisable today.

136.   The same view as photograph no. 135 but taken some 20 years later, and showing more clearly the shops on the south side of the High Street. Near right is Mr. T. Goss the saddler, then W. Price the butcher. Further along can be seen the Shell petrol sign at Mr. B. Thorne's garage business, which was competing for the emerging transport needs of the village; next is the greengrocer's and general grocery store of Mr. T. Griffin.

137.   Price's butcher's shop in the winter, around 1900. With snow lying on the ground there were few worries about the meat deteriorating whilst on display. Mr. Joseph Price established his business in Queen Street around 1870, but moved to these new premises at the centre of the village before the turn of the century. His original house and shop was the only building retained in Queen Street; after being given the "Rothschild treatment" it was named "The Limes" and was used thereafter as family accommodation for senior Manor staff.

138.   A reverse view to photograph no. 135, *circa* 1920. On the right can be seen the Primitive Methodist Chapel (built in 1876). At this time Waddesdon also had the Wesleyan Chapel, the Baptist Chapel in Frederick Street, and also a Baptist Chapel at Waddesdon Hill, which together with the parish church catered for the diverse spiritual needs of the village. Prior to the Great War all these churches were well attended and the rivalry between the non-Conformists and the Church of England members was intense.

139.   Another instantly recognisable view of the High Street, *circa* 1895. This picture is dominated by the house of Mr. H. Sherwin, one of the contractors employed by the Baron. It is said that the house, which was built in 1890, was largely constructed from materials "left over" from the Manor. The Baron arranged for the addition of the grand porch and upper level conservatory to improve the appearance of the house from the main road. (Note the unmade road.) At the left of picture, partly obscured by the lilac tree, is the butcher's shop of Mr. E. Newman, later to be taken over by Mr. S. Adams.

140.   The eastern junction of Baker Street and High Street, *circa* 1895, with the familiar "Bottom Shop", then an ale shop owned by the Aylesbury Brewery Company and operated by Phillips and Co. On the far side of the High Street are the business premises of Mr. Josiah Crook, general builders, van and cart makers, wheelwrights and undertakers. On the fence, far left of picture, can be seen the brass plate of Dr. Morrison, who was soon to move to the top end of the village.

141. Dr. Morrison's house and stable at the entrance to Britain Lane, *circa* 1895. With real horse-power as the only means of local transport for business and professional persons, it was the usual thing to have a stable and coach-house adjacent to the premises, and nearby a close for use as a paddock.

142. The "Bottom Shop", *circa* 1925, and run by Misses Figg and Moules. A general shop specialising in confectionery but also including "Ye Olde Corner Café" to attract the passing motorist (a rare thing in those days) and cyclists. On the wall is an advertisement for the Pavilion Cinema in Aylesbury, whilst a grand fête featuring an address by David Lloyd George in person is advertised in the shop window.

143.   It is hard to believe the photographer thought it worthwhile recording the Tea Garden of "Ye Olde Corner Café", but here it is. A possible candidate for the most boring postcard of 1925.

144.   The High Street from outside the "Bottom Shop", *circa* 1925. The garage business of Mr. David Evans can be seen at the left of picture just beyond the three-wheeler parked outside Figg and Moules' shop and café, which also advertised accommodation.

145. A quiet Sunday morning in 1925? A view down the High Street looking towards the "Bottom Shop". Adam's the butchers closed and not much sign of life elsewhere.

146. Back Road (Baker Street) looking towards the High Street, *circa* 1900. On the right is the rebuilt Bakers Arms. Down the road can be seen a loaded cart belonging to Mr. J. Robinson who was a "Haggle Carter" and who also hired out broughams (light, closed, four-wheeled horse-drawn carriage). Haggle Carters were general removal contractors, who carried anything from manure to bricks. (Note the unmade road.)

SCHOOLING AND SCHOOLS IN WADDESDON

The following details on the early days of schooling in the village have been gleaned from numerous sources, including the book *Waddesdon and Over Winchendon* by C. Oscar Morton. There has been a school in the village at least since the latter end of the 17th century. A book on Charity Schools in Bucks states that all children of the parish are "taught at the charges of the three Rectors, and other contributors". In 1691 an entry states that the overseers paid "Bigges Boyes schooling 1 yeare–8 shillings" (40p) and in the Waddesdon Baptismal Register for October 7 1701 there is mentioned "John the son of Richard Turner, Scholemaster, and Elizabeth his wife of this Towne".

In the early part of the 19th century the Rectors of the first and third portions allowed one pound annually for the schooling of two boys from the parish.

On September 12 1829 the Trustees of the Charity School passed a resolution requiring all boys of between 6 and 12 years, and receiving parish relief, to be sent to the School Room where a Mr. John Hitchcock was required to teach them all for the sum of 5 to 6 shillings (25–30p) per week.

Unfortunately no early photographs appear to exist of either the National or the British schools, so for the purposes of this book photographs nos 147 and 148 have been included although dating from later than 1925.

147.   The National School (Church School) from an aerial photograph taken in 1931. Here it can be seen with its extensive playgrounds just off Baker Street and more or less opposite The Grove. This school was built in 1910 when Miss Alice purchased the original National School which was situated near the entrance to the Manor grounds. As was the custom in those days the lavatories were constructed outside the building and at the extremities of the playground, the junior boys and all the girls on the right, and the senior boys on the left, the two groups separated by a fence across the playground. (© Hunting Aerofilms Ltd.)

The original National School was built on Church land near the centre of the old village, about 250 yards south of the church (see photograph no. 179). It was enlarged in 1860 and in that same year a school-house was added, in memory of the Rev. W. W. Walton. In 1846 a British School was constructed off Silk Street, providing teaching for the children of parents who preferred a non-sectarian education. In 1893 this school was condemned and a new British (Council) School was built in Baker Street, on Rothschild, land in 1894. In 1910 Miss Alice de Rothschild purchased the old National School for conversion to The Institute, and provided the land off Baker Street where the new National School was constructed from the proceeds of the sale. The new school capacity was for 170 pupils. See photograph no. 147.

During the 1970s the Church School was demolished and the Council School converted into apartments. New combined schools now serve in place of the two originals, situated on the land where for many years school allotments plots were used to teach boys the rudiments of gardening. See photograph no. 270.

148.   The British School (County School) photographed in the mid-1950s from the edge of "New Hall Pond". In 1894 the Bucks Education Department condemned the original British School near Silk Street and required the school managers to provide a new school for 250 pupils to be built in the course of 1895. The Baron chaired a public meeting, and a committee was elected to raise the money for the project. Mr. W. J. Taylor was the architect, and the lowest tenderer was Mr. C. Crook. The agreed figure for the work was £1,497.2s.0d. and the date for completion was to be 31 October 1895 (five months). Completion was delayed, partly due to variations, until December 1895, and the final cost of the completed project was just short of £2,000. Completing the school in little more than a year was an achievement by any standard and serves as an example of the organisation and energy which was everywhere in the village.

149.   Situated near to the Aylesbury Road in Humphrey's Ley, this fine looking windmill was a well-known landmark in the locality. Constructed for Miss Alice de Rothschild in 1905 near the site of a much earlier windmill, this one was more an ornamental than a practical machine. It was operated rent-free by Mr. J. Taylor, the village miller, when conditions were favourable. It is said that Miss Alice enjoyed seeing the sails turning as she travelled up the drive from the crossroads, and efforts were made to have the mill working when she returned to Waddesdon after prolonged absence. The original Aylesbury steeplechase started from Waddesdon Windmill on the 12th November 1834, and is thought to be the first ever steeplechase. The finishing post was one of Mr. Terry's fields near Aylesbury, in line with St Mary's church steeple.

In 1931 a series of aerial photographs (150 to 154) were taken to record the village of Waddesdon, and are published here by kind permission of Hunting Aerofilms Ltd, Borehamwood, Herts ©. They provide us with a unique "bench-mark" to compare progress from 1874 (photograph no. 1) to the modern day (photographs nos 266 to 271).

150. Waddesdon from the south. In the foreground is the National (Church) School, the Manor House (Atte Green) and farm buildings beyond it, whilst Frederick Street and Quainton Road stretch towards the top left of picture. In the centre can be seen the field known as "The Green", where for many years the annual Fair was held. At centre right the curve of Britain Lane points towards Britain House, lost amongst the trees.

151. The reverse of no. 150. This picture gives a unique view of Waddesdon's gas-works at the bottom end of Quainton Road, opposite the Mill (see photograph no. 154), also the tightly packed houses on the east side of Frederick Street, compared with the west side. In the distance the Estate parkland is clearly visible with the mature chestnut and elm trees in avenues and at field boundaries.

152.   Waddesdon from the west. Almost the whole village is included in this photograph when the aeroplane was over the Dairy in Queen Street. In the left foreground is the Estate yard and at bottom right is the driveway leading to the Manor. Already the woods at this end of the village have matured and envelop the area between Silk Street and Queen Street.

153.   Looking down onto the south face of the church this view is dominated by the Rothschild Estate plantations where the heart of the village had been only 50 years previously. In the background on the left are the two Parsons Closes with the small barn in the corner. The hedge at top left marks the line of the old London Road which by-passed the village for several hundred years.

154.   The lower end of Quainton Road showing the steam mill on one side, and opposite it the gas-works. This picture is an enlargment of a section of the aerial photograph (151) taken in 1931, and is the only known photograph of these two works. In its original location in Back Road, Mr. Joseph Taylor's steam mill had spoiled the Baron's view from the Manor. In due course Mr. Taylor was persuaded to forfeit the fresh water of the Wottesbroke for a 40-foot-deep well in Quainton Road. The water of course was essential for running the steam engine to turn the mill. The new mill was completed in 1893 and soon afterwards the site of the old mill was absorbed into the grounds of the Five Arrows Hotel. The Provincial Gas and Lighting Works Limited established their Quainton Road gasworks in 1883, and public buildings, larger houses, and street lights were able to receive "town gas" produced at the works. Poorer people still retained their paraffin lamps and solid fuel heating, i.e. coal and wood, but of course enjoyed the communal benefits of this facility. They were also welcome to purchase the coke and coal-tar by-products from the gas-making process. In 1916 the Manor's private gasworks at Westcott was closed down (see the following section) and a supply from the Waddesdon works was piped to the Manor, stables and laundry. This village gasworks became uneconomic and was closed down in the early 1930s.

SECTION FOUR

VILLAGE LIFE

Soon after work started on the Manor, local workers gained a great deal of satisfaction from an unsubstantiated account of how Mr. Treadwell, a tenant farmer and overseer of the poor, had complained to the Baron that he could not retain labour on the farm at 14 shillings per week if the Baron continued to offer jobs at 15 shillings. The Baron's advice had been "Well, pay them 16 shillings, Mr. Treadwell!"

By choosing to build his country house at Waddesdon and maintain it as his main residence, the new Lord of the Manor had improved the prospects of practically everyone in the locality. Regular wages, modern accommodation, and encouragement to participate in every possible uplifting activity, very quickly raised morale. Then of course there was the beneficial effect to the community of the influx of highly skilled workers, who often settled in the area, and Waddesdon news now featured regularly in the *Bucks Herald*.

The village organisations had a good neighbour who took a real interest in their well-being. In particular, larger projects such as the total rebuilding of the church tower and the provision of a new British School were completed in record time, thanks largely to the financial support and encouragement of the Baron. In 1897 the Baron provided the splendid Village Hall as a venue for cultural and social activities.

However, it was the Baron's Annual Treat which the villagers anticipated, and remembered with pleasure long into their old age. The Treats were organised for the workers and villagers, but as time passed the number of visitors increased by hundreds, and all flocked to the Manor grounds to enjoy the bands and funfair.

By the early 1900s Waddesdon had everything from tap water to a brand-new sewerage system, street lighting, and a village hall.

The Baron's sister Miss Alice had carried on his traditions and added a few of her own, including the annual Christmas Party (with moving-picture show) for all the children, the Waddesdon Sports Day and Miss Alice's Tea Party (formerly "The Treat"). Older traditions such as the annual Feast Day at Michealmas-tide and the seven-yearly event of Beating the Bounds had been retained. Waddesdon had two Brass Bands, a Philharmonic and Operatic Society, and successful Football and Cricket Clubs.

The Great War of 1914–18 saw the same young men who had dominated the local sporting scene, marching off to join the armed forces. Of these, 62 were "killed in action", and the effect on the village was devastating. A memorial to their sacrifice was constructed on Waddesdon's only remaining portion of common land, the old Green or Square.

It is said that almost every aspect of life changed because of the Great War, and possibly nowhere more so than Waddesdon. A different normality evolved, more in keeping perhaps with the 20th century, and although still of vital importance to the local economy, the Manor and Estate would never again employ so many people.

Different standards would prevail in the light of the economics of the age, but the villagers persevered with their social interests, gaining more than average success. Waddesdon Cricket Club was still admired in the locality, the Football Club was still winning trophies and by 1925 was back to its eminent position of the early 1900s.

The photographs gathered for this section illustrate the numerous aspects of life during the period 1874–1925. In this rather spick-and-span village there was an aura of confidence and contentment which reflected the situation. The people had experienced much worse, and things had improved dramatically; they had competed and often won.

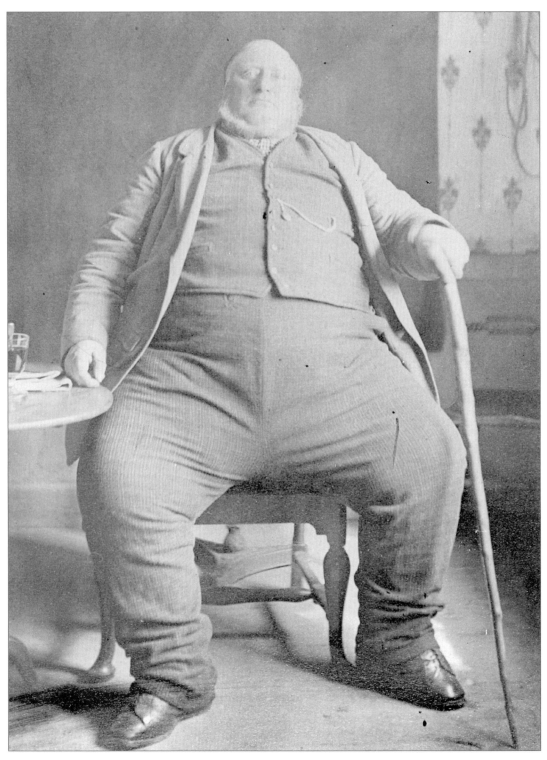

155.   The "Waddesdon Giant" – William Stevens – a legend from pre-Rothschild days, who died at the age of 46 on Good Friday, March 31 1877. Previously the tenant farmer at Lodge Hill, at the time of his death Mr. Stevens was residing at the Five Arrows Inn (Marlborough Arms). His enormous appetite was renowned and his weight was reputed to be 38 stones. He died after consuming a large breakfast of bacon and sausages followed by numerous hot-cross buns. The problem of removing his body from the inn was solved by taking out one of the bow windows.

THE DAY SCHOOL.

Our readers will be glad to know that Mrs. Lay has obtained the post of Schoolmistress at Cublington, in this County, where we trust she may find a comfortable and happy home ; our good wishes will accompany her. The fund for the benefit of herself and her little ones is now over £80. The Committee have elected Mr. and Mrs. Tinsley, from Walsden, Lancashire, as successors of Mr. and Mrs. Lay. They come to us with very high recommendations, which we have no doubt they will be able to justify by their efficient management of our School. Mr. Tinsley was trained at Saltley College, and has a First Class Certificate : he holds his full D., and four Science Certificates. Mr. Tinsley will also act as organist. We sincerely hope their residence here may be happy for themselves, and of benefit to our parish.

SCHOOL TREAT.

On Wednesday, the 19th, Baron F. de Rothschild entertained the Waddesdon and Winchendon Schools, with the parents, teachers, and many of the inhabitants, at his new house, henceforth to be called "Waddesdon Manor." About 1500 were present. There was a shower of rain just when the long procession started, but very soon the sunshine returned, and the rest of the day was very fine. The Aylesbury band led the way ; the little ones went in waggons, the older children and parents walking in procession, including a strong contingent of the Night School. The effect of the long procession, as it approached the tents, was very striking. The Baron, accompanied by several friends of his own, including Lord Rosebery, was present. Mrs. Dodwell provided an excellent tea, and some of the company, we heard, were regaled with wine to drink the Baron's health, and wish him long enjoyment of his splendid house. During the afternoon, a composition of Mr. Thomas Garner was sung in honour of the Baron. The Rector offered him the thanks of the visitors, and he responded in a short speech, in which he announced that he should hope each year to entertain his neighbours in the same way. There was an excellent Punch and Judy and performing dogs. Dancing, round games, and races were indulged in, and at about 8 o'clock the large party broke up. The night before, there was a fine display of fireworks, and the house was brilliantly illuminated ; the effect from a distance was very beautiful.

156. The Parish Magazine of June 1880 included this report of the very first "Treat" given by the Baron to the children and inhabitants of Waddesdon and Winchendon. This special occasion was to be repeated annually although the date in May was subsequently changed in favour of a day in August. The "Baron's Treat" became "the day" for youngsters in the locality, and the number of all ages attending increased year by year.

157.   After the Baron's death in 1898 there was just one more "Treat" on the scale of those previously held. This was in 1899 when thousands of people flocked to Waddesdon on 8 August to enjoy the holiday entertainment and watch the athletic sports held for the school children of Waddesdon, Westcott and Upper Winchendon. Special trains were laid on by the Metropolitan Railway Company and many villagers earned extra cash by providing bicycle parking and teas for the visitors. The crowd was estimated to be around 20,000. This photograph of 1910 shows the procession of school-children preceded by the Temperance Silver Band, marching to the Manor grounds for the annual Athletic Sports and Tea Party. This event had taken the place of the old "Treat", and was limited by invitation to inhabitants of the three villages.

158.   All the fun of the fair at the "Baron's Treat" 1897. This year the villagers enjoyed an additional Treat when the occasion of Queen Victoria's Diamond Jubilee was celebrated on June 22. The Jubilee "Treat' was restricted to villagers only, and a mere 1,000 persons were entertained to lunch by the Baron. The day was packed with memorable activities, including Ye Olde English Sports, a bun-eating competition, greasy pole, several bands, an excellent tea for 600 children, medals, demonstrations, comic cricket, fancy dress, costume cycle parade followed by an illuminated procession, and the day was rounded off with a firework display, supplied by Brock and Son of the Crystal Palace, held in front of the Five Arrows Hotel.

159. Preparing Miss Alice's Party, *circa* 1912. Mr. Phil Dodwell in the flat cap at the right of the photograph was the caterer on this occasion. On alternate years it would be Mr. T. Franklin. Traditionally each family in the village was supplied with an appropriate number of free teas and free fun-fair tickets prior to the big day. The "Treat" commenced when the children gathered at their respective schools, formed up in procession and marched to Spring Hill field. The National School was headed by the Temperance Band, and the British School by the Old Prize Band. A wide range of athletic sports were vigorously contested, with cash prizes, the bands played, the gardens were open for inspection and tea was arranged for everyone. The day was pleasantly completed by yet more music and dancing on the grass.

160. Helpers at Miss Alice's Party, *circa* 1913. This large number of men and women were employed by the caterers, either Mr. Dodwell or Mr. Franklin, to prepare and serve the afternoon tea-party for the ticket holders from Waddesdon, Winchendon and Westcott. *Front row sitting*: Mrs. H. Oliffe, Mrs. H. Holland, Miss P. Saunders, Miss K. Fowler, —, —, Mrs. C. Fowler, Mr. R. Franklin, Mrs. S. Franklin, Mr. T. Franklin, Mrs. S. Radwell, Mrs. R. Copcutt, Mrs. Palmer, —, —, —. *Second row standing*: Mr. Jim Atkins, Mr. Bert Cripps, —, —, Mr. C. Skinner, Mr. R. Crook, Mr. W. Walton, Mr. G. Evans, Mr. J. West, —, —, Mr. H. Oliffe, Mr. C. Hicks, Mr. W. Uff. *Back row*: —, —, —, —, Mr. C. Gale, —, Mr. H. Gilson, Mr. W. Harding, Mr. J. Allen, —, Mr. H. Taylor, —.

161.   After the procession of school-children had made its way to the Treat, there followed the remainder of the villagers as shown in this photograph of around 1910. The shop at the centre of the picture is Mr. Dodwell's general store mentioned earlier in this book. The shop-front at left of centre displayed the wares of Edwin Garner, shoemaker. Mr. Garner was probably well known though as a key member of the Philharmonic Society "String Band".

162.   A section of the crowd for the prize-giving ceremony at the Waddesdon Athletic Sports, *circa* 1905. This photograph was taken from the balcony roof of the Cricket Pavilion.

163.   Coronation Day celebrations June 22 1911. The village football ground in Britain Field provided the venue for sports and fun to mark the coronation of George V. Judging by the umbrellas in the photograph the weather could have been better. However, the large crowd had plenty to enjoy with a free tea and dancing to the village bands to follow. The chimney of Taylors' steam mill provides a prominent landmark in Quainton Road.

164.   The ladies' egg and spoon race at the Coronation sports in Britain Field, exciting considerable interest from the officials on the sideline. June 22 1911.

165.   Competitors in a cycle race at the Waddesdon Athletic Sports held in the Cricket Field, *circa* 1910. Although a village holiday, it is quite clear that it was also a day for "Sunday best" clothes, for the spectators.

166.   An amusing part of an obstacle race providing the village photographer with the challenge of an unposed and moving subject for the record, *circa* 1910.

167 and 168.   The four-yearly Olympic Games which had commenced as the Modern Olympics in 1896 awakened a popular interest in athletics, and in particular the marathon. In the early 1900s an annual race from Bicester to Aylesbury attracted the crowds *en route*. These photographs record the passage of the competitors in Waddesdon's wide High Street near the Five Arrows Hotel and also at the corner near to the "Bottom Shop", *circa* 1905.

169.   For most of the 25 years before the outbreak of war in 1914 Waddesdon F.C. was amongst the most successful clubs in the locality. A founder member of the Oving and District Villages Association in 1889, Waddesdon none-the-less had to wait until 1898 to win the "Oving Cup". Having won it once, Waddesdon went on to win it again in 1899. Thereafter the Oving Villages Cup was often amongst the trophies on display by successive victorious Waddesdon teams, and was always the most coveted by players and supporters alike. This photograph shows a proud Waddesdon team at the verandah of the Cricket Pavilion in 1899. On the table is the original Oving Cup to be held by Waddesdon for a year after defeating Oving F.C. by five goals to two. Standing at the far left is a very young Harry Gilson, who was to feature in so many successful Waddesdon teams during the next 15 years.

170. Tradesmen's XI. This photograph reflects the confident atmosphere which prevailed in 1907. The fact that Waddesdon should have sufficient shop-keepers to field a football team of any standard is now difficult to comprehend. However, neither the opposing team nor this occasion is listed in the record books so we assume it was a friendly game staged purely for pleasure. *Sitting on fence*: Harry Crook, —, Harry Dodwell, John Grace, John Adams. *Standing*: Ewart Newman, —, —, Mr. Humphry, Fred Crook, Thomas Franklin, Sid Crook.

171. The first XI, *circa* 1910, once again at the Cricket Pavilion but this time showing the stairway, at left, leading to the viewing area on the flat roof. *Rear standing*: —, S. Dexter, H. Gilson, E. Timms. *Middle standing*: T. Franklin, J. Saunders, W. Saunders, —, E. Creed, C. Adams, G. Richards, L. Copcutt. *Front seated*: F. Cannon, W. Ewers, C. Cox, J. Hillesdon. *Front*: —, W. Lane.

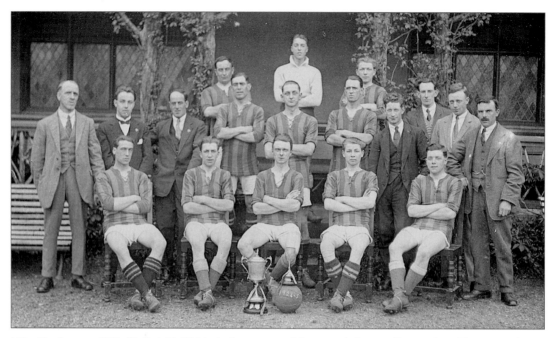

172.   The first team 1924–25. Probably Waddesdon's most successful team, and all were village residents. They were unbeaten in the Aylesbury District League and shared the cup with R.A.F. Halton after three successive drawn "deciders". Just as important was the win in the Oving Village Cup for the second successive year, and especially this time in beating Quainton 3–2. *Standing, left to right*: W. Whitney, G. Atkins, R. Wood, G. Finch, G. Ewers, G. Rolfe, J. Gilson (Goalkeeper), F. Winchcomb, F. Edridge, F. Cripps, A. Hicks, E. Southam, T. Mole. *Seated*: G. Cannon, F. Eldridge, J. Rolfe (Captain), W. Eldridge, E. Atkins.

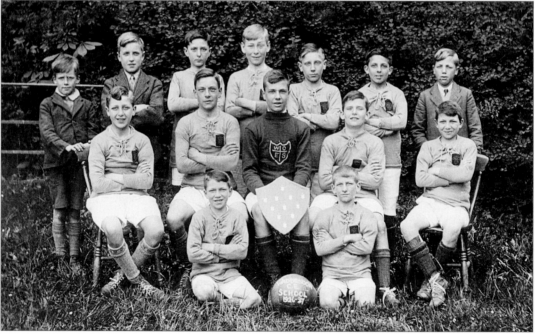

173.   The National School team of 1927. *Back row*: Harold Goss, Ron Whitney, Jim Collyer, Frank Howe, Bob Snelling, Arthur Crook, Les Burgess. *Middle row*: Reg Baker, Cyril Copcutt, Frank Hinton, Lionel George, Jack Eldridge. *Front row*: Laurie Eldridge, Den Eldridge. Success in local school football was to be succeeded by success in the Aylesbury District League for several of these players, notably the Eldridge brothers, who became well known for sporting prowess.

174.   Play in progress at the Cricket Field, *circa* 1910. Starting in humble circumstances in 1878, the Cricket Club was without a ground for its first season and went more than two years without a win. However, under the patronage of the Baron and later Miss Alice de Rothschild the club soon had a field, a pavilion, and a groundsman. Success on the field, which incidentally was the best village ground in the vicinity, was bound to follow. In 1907 Miss Alice provided the Tea Room shown here alongside the Pavilion, and about that time extensive ground improvements were carried out. These facilities together with good ground-keeping and a proficient membership established Waddesdon Cricket Club in the fixture list of teams from far and wide. Games against London teams as well as Aylesbury Town and Leighton Buzzard were regularly played at Waddesdon before the First World War.

175.   The Royal and Central Agricultural Association Show was the forerunner of the Bucks County Show. Originally there was no permanent showground and the venue was usually different each year. Wherever the show was held, the local businesses benefited. In 1891 the show was first held in the Manor grounds and again in 1896, under the Presidency of Baron F.J. de Rothschild M.P. The cutting from the *Bucks Herald* of Saturday 25 July 1896 shows how Waddesdon's two hotels took the opportunity to advertise their services. Of additional interest is the second advertisement for the White Lion – this time for the Baron's Treat. It shows that the Waddesdon Schools' Treat had evolved into a treat for visitors as well, not to mention a bumper day for village businesses.

ROYAL & CENTRAL BUCKS
AGRICULTURAL SHOW, WADDESDON,
THURSDAY NEXT, JULY 30th, 1896.

FIVE ARROWS HOTEL,
WADDESDON.

EXHIBITORS AT THE SHOW wanting
BOXES or STALLS at the above HOTEL
are requested to make early application.

Loose Boxes, Stalls, &c.
STOCK, &c., SPECIALLY PROVIDED FOR

☞ LUNCHEONS AND TEAS CAN BE HAD
AT ANY TIME DURING THE DAY.

HY. TURNHAM,
PROPRIETOR.

ROYAL & CENTRAL BUCKS
AGRICULTURAL SHOW, WADDESDON,
THURSDAY NEXT, JULY 30th, 1896.

WHITE LION HOTEL,
WADDESDON.

GEORGE COCKERILL,
PROPRIETOR of the above HOTEL, has
made SPECIAL ARRANGEMENTS for every
ACCOMMODATION at the SHOW.

GOOD LOOSE BOXES, STALLS, &c.
Which should be secured early.

EXCELLENT ACCOMMODATION FOR STOCK.

☞ Luncheons, Teas, &c., provided at any time

BARON F. DE ROTHSCHILD, M.P.'s
SCHOOL TREAT, WADDESDON
TUESDAY, AUGUST 4th, 1896,

GOOD ACCOMMODATION
WILL BE FOUND AT
THE WHITE LION HOTEL.

Refreshments at Moderate Charges.

Good Standings for Horses and Vehicles

PROPRIETOR—
GEORGE COCKERILL.

176.   The Bucks Show on the lower slopes of Lodge Hill in 1909. An idyllic setting with the backdrop formed by the now maturing trees, and, just visible, the village church. The entrance to the showground, on the left of picture beyond the flagpole, was adjacent to the main drive leading to the Manor.

177.   The main ring at the Bucks Show 1909. This view looking towards the Cricket Field is an interesting study of an Edwardian function in a rural setting. A few motor cars are positioned at the ring-side, the crowd is absorbed in the entertainment and the ladies appear to be as well turned out as any competitor.

178.   Another photograph of the 1909 Bucks Show, with this time a competitor's view from inside the main ring whilst the trade turnouts are showing their paces. The pony and trap on the left was owned and driven by Mr. H. Turnham the landlord of the Five Arrows Hotel (see photograph no. 191), whilst the turnout at the centre is Mr. Fred Evans, the local coal merchant. (See photograph no. 192.)

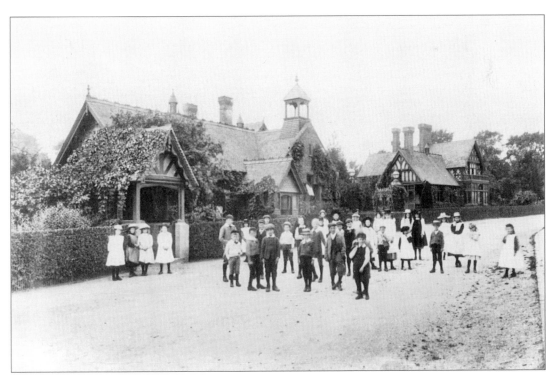

179.   Schoolchildren outside the National School providing a somewhat incongruous reception for the grand visitors to the Manor; though no doubt they were always on their best behaviour at such times! *Circa* 1905.

180.   Raising the Union Jack at the Nation School on St George's Day, *circa* 1900. The chestnut trees are in blossom and all the schoolchildren have turned out in their best attire to salute the flag.

181.   The Sunday School class at the Methodist chapel, *circa* 1900. The superintendent, Mr. Harry Larby, standing at the rear in the centre, also assisted at the evening classes which were held at the National School. Built in 1876, the chapel enjoyed only around 50 years in its intended role, and was eventually converted into the garage workshop of Mr. W. Rhodes.

182. A group of scholars at the British School, with Mr. Rushden the headmaster around, *circa* 1905. The village population consisted of roughly equal numbers of Church of England and "Chapel" families. The Church of England children attended the National School whilst the Free Church children attended the British School. *Back row, left to right*: George Copcutt, Harry Cripps, Jack Wheeler, Fred Stanton, George Ewers, Alf Fowler, Ron Crook, Ralph Rolfe, Ralph Saunders, Stan Biswell, Fred Cripps, Mr. Rushden. *Row 2*: Lionel Cannon, Jack Rolfe, Alf Fowler, Bert Saunders, G. Stanton, Rufus Fowler, Ted Sharp, Hubert Biswell, Stan Southam, Henry Thorpe, Horace Saunders, Maurice Saunders. *Row 3*: Annie Pollard, Ethel Atkins, Florie Price, Jess Figg, Lilly Blake, May Atkins, Alice Allen. *Row 4*: Min Copcutt, Em Southam, Nell Church, Ethel Sharp, Bessie Evans, Annie Biswell, Winnie Ford, Daisy George. *Front row 5*: John Thorpe, May Allen, Win Sharp, Charlie George, Madge Thorpe, Elsie George, Alice George. Ten years later many of the boys had joined the armed forces and by the end of the war five had been killed in action.

183.   The infant class of 1911 in the new national (Church of England) School. This school, built as a result of Miss Alice acquiring the original school and school house at the entrance to the Manor grounds, incorporated the latest ideas. The large high-ceilinged classrooms benefited from maximum daylight thanks to the many windows; the rooms were separated by folding partitions which were easily operated; and perhaps the most welcome of all was the central heating system powered from an underground boiler. As can be seen from this photograph there was a militaristic image (for the photographer at least), under the headmaster, Mr. Camp. Discipline was strict, but every effort was made to encourage scholastic success. Regular attendance at both village schools was rewarded by presentation of prizes provided by Miss Alice de Rothschild. These unique gifts comprised of compact wooden writing chests for the boys, and sewing boxes for the girls; things to be treasured for many long years.

184.   The infant class of 1925 at the Council (British) School. *Back row*: Ena Sharp, Evelyn Scott, Arthur Cheshire, Les Fowler, Glad Holland, Vera Taylor, Ted Ewers, Josie Fowler, Cyril Biswell. *Front row*: Bern Holland, Harry Carr, Jean Radwell, Bob Read, Marg Harding, Madge Walker.

185.   A junior class at the Council School, *circa* 1925. *L to R*: "Ginger" Bailey, Alf Taylor, Charlie Cripps, Jack George, Vic Sharp, Lloyd Walker, Fred Carter, Jack Scott, Oliver Franklin, —, Gerald Heplethwait, Arthur Copcutt, Valda Creed, Murray Cannon, Harry Biswell, Dolly Harding, Marg Saunders, Doris Rodwell, —, Eva Biswell.

186.   The entrance to Baker Street, formerly Back Road, *circa* 1902. The hay cart on the right probably belonged to Mr. J. Robinson who lived opposite the Bakers Arms. He was a "Haggle Carter" (transporter of all types of materials) by trade and also let out broughams for hire. During the early years of construction of the Manor it was not unusual for every available horse and cart in the village to be employed on the works. The Bakers Arms standing in the background had been run by John Dymock since 1877, and was to trade under successive landlords of the Dymock family until the 1970s. The "front-room" shop on the left was one of many such businesses which provided a wide range of small goods such as sewing material and sweets, for the immediate neighbourhood.

187.   The "Bottom Shop" in its original guise. This shop and several nearby houses were built for the Aylesbury Brewery Company in the late 19th century. It is evident this photograph was taken on the same day as no. 186. At the doorway to the shop is Mr. George Sharp the wheelwright, whilst the same children are posing for the photographer as in the previous study. At the centre of the picture is one of the gas street lights which helped to set Waddesdon apart from almost all the neighbouring villages at this time.

188.   Price's butcher's delivery cart with Mr. "Will" Uff in the driving seat. It is thought this photograph was taken at Quainton *circa* 1900, a time when nearly all the Waddesdon shopkeepers enjoyed the patronage of neighbouring villages and farmsteads.

189. Franklin's delivery "van" with Mr. Tommy Franklin standing by the wheel, *circa* 1905. Every shop selling provisions had to cater for local farms and hamlets by delivering weekly to their customers. In Waddesdon the principal stores all had bakeries which necessitated daily deliveries known as "bread-rounds". Franklin's was probably the most successful bread-round in the village, not only by virtue of selling the most bread but also displaying at the shop the numerous trophies won at competitions.

190. The milk collection cart on its way to Waddesdon Manor Station, *circa* 1915. Mr. Collyer the tailor was still in business; the Coffee Tavern next door had long since become a private dwelling.

191.   Mr. Henry Turnham, landlord of the Five Arrows Hotel, proudly showing off his trade turnout in the yard prior to the judging at the Bucks Show, held that year in the Manor grounds, 1909. (See photograph no. 178.)

192.   Mr. Fred Evans delivering coal to 72 Quainton Road, *circa* 1912. Mr. Evans enjoyed considerable success in the trade turnout section of local shows when his working outfit was specially prepared for the judges' eyes. (See photograph no. 178.) A family concern, F.T. Evans and Son has continued in business to the present time.

193.   Waddesdon's very first motor car, built by the driver Mr. David Evans in 1899, and registered in 1903 (BH 80). Mr. Evans lived at number 14 High Street, a small terraced house, and it was here that he constructed his three-wheeled, single cylinder motor car. An engineer and mechanic to his finger-tips, Mr. Evans gained an excellent reputation, both locally and amongst enthusiasts from afar. William Morris, later to become the founder of Morris Motors, Cowley, was a frequent visitor on his motor-cycle combination. The Evans family first came to Waddesdon in 1875, when David's father, William Evans, a millwright, was recruited to operate the steam winch which was used to haul the building materials up the slope of Lodge Hill for the construction of the Manor. Engineering and mechanical expertise has since then always been associated with the Evans family and remains so to this day.

194.   In the early 1900s David Evans manufactured and sold stationary engines to farmers in the locality, and later on he assembled commercial engines, principally the American Amanco horizontal single cylinder two-and-a-half H.P. During the Great War, 90 of these engines were sold to local farmers. This photograph shows David Evans with his young son Sam exhibiting a typical stationary engine of the post-war period, whilst in the foreground is a model of a horizontal engine; no doubt David's handiwork. Sam eventually took over the business and carried on the Evans's tradition in Waddesdon.

195.   Coal delivery, probably to Mr. Collyer, *circa* 1910. The men were employed by Mr. Turnham of the Five Arrows Hotel, who along with other businessmen in the village would purchase coal by the waggon-load. This would have been delivered to Waddesdon Road Station near Hall Farm (see photograph no. 203) and then hauled in carts to the buyers' homes.

196.   This smartly attired young man poses proudly with his new motorcycle which displays the registration number A1467 circa 1910.

197.   Another young person smartly dressed and with her motor-cycle. Miss Pratt worked at the Manor and was obviously a self-assured young lady who was eager to demonstrate her independence, *circa* 1912.

198.   Mr. Henry Turnham was "seeing off" his guests in this Spyker open tourer after their rather eventful visit to the Five Arrows Hotel. During the visit the car developed a fault which necessitated attention by David Evans, who had to manufacture a back axle component to allow the car to continue its journey, *circa* 1912.

199.   Dr. Morrison at the wheel of his Humber, *circa* 1910. The ladies are dressed in typical Edwardian motoring apparel. The village doctor had by now settled at "The Roses", the specially built house overlooking the village square, having previously practised at the other end of the village, next door to Crook's the undertakers!

200.   Mr. Cyril Goss with his wife Emily beside him and with six additional passengers, *circa* 1913. Cyril was a keen driver who spent many of his working years driving buses out of Aylesbury.

201. Mr. Fred Paxton, landlord of the White Lion Hotel, proudly demonstrating his new car to his friends whilst Mrs. Paxton (in hat) looks on.

202. Steam horsepower on the Brill Tramway around 1900. The engine was a Manning Wardle manufactured in Leeds and purchased in 1894. The lady is Mary Varney, who was the level-crossing gate-keeper at Westcott. On the foot-plate is Harry Cross the driver, with fireman Arthur Bayliss. At the right of picture can be seen the waiting room/ticket office of Westcott Station (still standing in 1995). Although by this time the transporting of building materials for the Manor was a distant memory, the rail traffic to Westcott was enhanced by the activities of the Manor gas-works, which was supplied via a branch line at Wescott. (© London Transport Museum.)

203.   Waddesdon Road Station on the Quainton to Brill Tramway. The station was on the north side of the Waddesdon to Westcott road at Rag Hall and clearly shows the siding used for the unloading of coal trucks as mentioned in caption no. 195. Lodge Hill can be seen in the left background, and the cottage, which is part of Hall Farm, seen here behind the crossing gate on the south side of the road (A41) still stands (1995). (© London Transport Museum.)

204.   The hand-bell team on New Year's Eve *circa* 1912. *Standing*: Win Walton, Charlie Skinner, Harry Allen, Ernie Slade. *Sitting*: Frank Brackley, Jack Allen. Photographed in village photographer Albert Cherry's back garden, alongside the old Wesleyan Chapel, this team of bell ringers would visit local farms and cottages, playing carols and taking considerable liquid refreshment, such that on their return to the village the music was suffering but the players were oblivious to criticism!

205.   The Waddesdon Prize Band or "Old Band" as it was known, photographed in front of the Cricket Pavilion, *circa* 1908. The "Old Band" was certainly in existence in the 1860s and by the early 1900s was probably announcing its contest-winning achievements by incorporating "Prize" in its title. *Back row*: Jim Cook, Eli Cripps, Teddy Fowler. *Middle row*: Tom Sharp, Alf Fowler, Harry Ewers, Walt Biswell, Herbert Owen, W. Fowler (senior). *Sitting*: Will Fowler, R. Allen, C. Cripps (Guest Conductor), Will Fowler, Harry Cripps, Stan Biswell, Sid Biswell, George Biswell. *Front*: Frank Cripps, Hubert Biswell.

206.   Wesleyan School Treat 1907. Not quite as grand as the annual Church Choir outing which for many years had visited various seaside resorts or sometimes London, the Wesleyan School Treat was nonetheless eagerly anticipated by everyone concerned. In those days, when most people rarely left the village boundaries, community pleasures were heightened by "treats" such as this. The Wesleyan Chapel had for more than 100 years been second only to the Church of England in membership and had always put considerable effort into its Sunday School. The Treat commenced on the chosen day with a gathering at around 2.00 pm at the Sunday School, then preceded by the Temperance Silver Band everyone marched to the field (Warmstone in this case). At the front of the marching scholars, four of the older children carried the School Banner. During the afternoon races and games were organised, everyone receiving sweets, then tea, as can be seen in this photograph, and finally marching back to the old Sunday School where each pupil received a freshly baked currant bun from Franklin's Bakery. A simple but much-loved event which the participants remembered for many years.

207. By 1925 the normal venue for the Wesleyan Treat was at the Cricket Field. Here we see the Sunday School teachers and "treat helpers" in front of the Cricket Pavilion. *Rear left to right*: J. Atkins, B. Sharp, J. Thorp, B. Crook. H. Crook. *Middle*: T. Ewers, ——, N. Hicks, W. Sharp, ——, Mrs. Taylor, C. Sharp, D. Cripps, A. Holland. *Front*: F. Southam, Mrs. C. Hicks, Mrs. B Sharp, Mrs. M. Crook, Mrs. Harding, Mrs. Fowler, ——, Mr. Gibbs.

208. An outing preparing to leave from outside the Primitive Methodist Chapel, *circa* 1905. Seated with the reins in the first wagonette is Mr. Henry Turnham, landlord of the Five Arrows Hotel and provider of hired transport. The brick wall at the right encloses the builder's yard of Mr. H. H. Sherwin at 30 High Street.

209.   The Waddesdon Philharmonic Society annually performed to packed audiences in the Village Hall. Mr. S. C. Camp A.R.C.O., headmaster of the National School, was not only the conductor of the "String Band" but also directed the performances in the comic operas and musical variety evenings. Great efforts were made to ensure success, including costumes and scenery hired from London. The village boasted many good singers and actors who in these circumstances were encouraged to extend their abilities to the full, not least these performers from an operetta, *circa* 1910. Second left is T. Franklin, sixth left is W. Walton, and far left is Winnie Camp (daughter of S. C. Camp).

210.   Waddesdon Temperance Silver Band photographed at the entrance porch of the village hall around 1910. Music and making music was high on the list of most popular pastimes in the village. From hymn singing to Gilbert and Sullivan performances by the Philharmonic Society, from Morris dances to the latest military marches, the community certainly knew its music. The Temperance Band practised at the Wesleyan Chapel, which was known as the Sunday School Room and strangely had a majority of C of E members, who on occasions were more temperate by name than by nature!

211. Jimmy Jones in the new uniform of the Temperance Silver Band. This smart young man is shown here at the age of about 12 years, photographed in Mr. Albert Cherry's studio, *circa* 1912. Jimmy Jones later became the proprietor of a garage workshop and shop opposite the Alms houses, and remained in business until the 1970s.

212. Waddesdon Morris Men in rather motley garb. Not too much is known about this village pastime in Waddesdon, except that the group regularly performed at Rectory Fêtes and the music was usually provided by Mr. "Billy" Uff on the fiddle. *Left to right*: Will Franks, Jack Uff, Win Walton, Randall Styles, —-, —, *circa* 1920.

213.   On the occasion of their silver wedding anniversary the Rev. and Mrs. Farmer held a tea party to which all the older people were invited. This photograph shows that a good response resulted and a most enjoyable time was had by all. In the centre of the photograph, with his arms folded, is the Rev. Farmer, on his right in the boater is his brother, and to his left is Mrs. Farmer and their son. *Back row*: C. Richards, Mrs. L. Brackley, Miss Webber, H. Olliffe, J. Goss, Dr. and Mrs. Morrison, Rev. Scott, Mrs. Olliffe. *Front row sitting*: —, Mrs. K. Cripps, —, Mrs. Slade, Mrs. Biswell, Mrs. Phillips, Elijah Collier, Mrs. Cowley. *Sitting on grass*: Mrs. Gibbons, Mrs. Walters, Mrs. Pickering, Mrs. Carrick.

214.   The tea-party in full swing. Perhaps by modern-day standards the seats could be a little more comfortable.

215.   The welfare of the villagers was a subject on which Miss Alice de Rothschild expected to be continuously informed, and as a result she endeavoured to ensure that those who fell on hard times received practical help. This photograph records an occasion when Mr. Wildridge, an estate official, paid out to deserving people on the instructions of Miss Alice gifts to assist in the purchase of the essentials of life. Mr. Wildridge, in the boater, was a popular man and a "bit of a card", having the temerity to smile at the camera! Behind him is Elijah Collyer, and in the shadows at right rear is Balem Cripps. The boy is Harry Cripps, who was collecting the gift for his grandmother Kitty Cripps. The venue is the back entrance to the Village Hall and the date is around 1905.

216.   George Sharp's wheelwright workshop was established at the newly built number 1 High Street in 1885, and he proceeded to build a reputation for hard work, good craftsmanship and integrity. His products ranged from ordinary wheel-barrows to the famous Oxfordshire Waggons, ladders of all dimensions, and of course repairs to keep older waggons working. He was a true rural craftsman who manufactured everything from raw materials. Standing elm trees were bought, felled, sawn and seasoned for timber, and iron bar was fashioned into all manner of fittings. Iron tyres for wheels, heated in an open fire of wood and sawdust then shrunk onto the wooden rims of the wheels, were all made by Mr. Sharp and his sons. At this time a wheelwright was essential to village life and Waddesdon had two, as George's brother Tom was in business in Frederick Street. Photographed here is Mr. Sharp, with axe on shoulder, and two of his sons, Ted and Bob, surrounded by examples of their work, *circa* 1911.

217.   In the early 1900s the Liberal Party campaigned to reform the Poor Laws and to introduce in their place the first old age pensions. The Baron had been the Liberal Member of Parliament for this constituency and after his death the seat was held by the Hon. L. W. Rothschild. In this photograph we have two young supporters in the General Election of January 1906 posing outside the Village Hall, and probably not having to do too much to secure the votes of the majority of the village electorate. The girl on the right is Holly Evans, the daughter of engineer David Evans

218.   The Boer War of 1899–1902 saw the call-up of militia and reservists to enable the armed forces to meet the demands made upon them. Waddesdonians who were thus involved included Messrs Simms, Lander, and Biswell; thankfully they all returned safely. The villagers welcomed them back in style. This "Welcome Home" arch was just part of it. The cutting from the Waddesdon Deanery Magazine describes the arrival home of George (Musical George) Biswell. A light-hearted thanksgiving which was to be unthinkable in the different circumstances of 1918.

219.   Cutting from Waddesdon Parish Magazine.

220.   The Church of England Men's Society, *circa* 1912. Photographed at the doorway to the Rectory this fine assembly includes many of the businessmen of the village, amongst them Albert Cherry, Phil Dodwell, Henry Turnham, and Alfred Collier. Sitting with arms folded is the Rector, the Rev. Farmer. The strong membership of this Society was typical for most organisations in the village, reflecting the healthy state of community life at that time.

221.   Tommy Griffin's mother set up a green-grocery shop in the front room of their house at 33 Frederick Street, but by the early 1920s the business had transferred to these premises, which had previously been Tom Saunders' shoe-maker's shop. Here we see Mr. and Mrs. T. Griffin at their newly decorated establishment in the High Street, *circa* 1924. Mr. Griffin survived in business despite being the "softest touch" for all the penniless children in the village, a gentleman in every way.

222.   Mr. Phillip Dodwell in his trap outside his shop at 92 High Street, *circa* 1910. Waddesdon's smart High Street of that period is illustrated at close quarters in this photograph, the cobbled path with not a weed in sight and the prosperous grocery shop behind its wrought-iron fencing. At the left-hand window can be seen the remains of the original Post Office sign, the Post Office itself having been removed to Humphrey's shop a few dozen yards away. In those days, when the slightest misdemeanour in the Post Office was dealt with very severely, Dodwell's lost the franchise when they failed to deliver circulars sent through the mail. A scandal which was only mentioned in private!

223.   When the Liberal government introduced the first old age pension in 1908, those who received it had to show that their income was less than £21 per year, in which case they received 5 shillings (25p), or 10 shillings (50p) if married. For those whose annual income was more than £21 but less than £31 a reduced pension was paid. This scheme relieved the local Board of Guardians, who had been responsible for administering aid to the poor of the parish since 1834. This photograph records the very first payment of the old age pension at Humphrey's shop, which by now was also the village Post Office. Mr. Humphreys was yet another grocer and baker at a time when Waddesdon was blessed with six. *Sitting, left to right*: Kitty Cripps, David Howe, Mrs. Higgins, Mrs. Copcutt. *Standing, front row*: Mrs. Quarrendon, Frankie Taylor, Ester Harding, Mrs. Alcock, Mrs. T. Biswell, Amos Buckle, Ted Hicks, Sam George. *Back row*: Mr. Cripps, Ben Marlow, Thomas Radwell, Mrs. Pearson, William Venemore, Mrs. Carrick, Mr. Basten (pension payer), Mrs. Walsh, Balem Cripps, Mr. Saunders, Thomas Biswell, Mr. Fowler.

224. Harvesting a field of barley by hand, *circa* 1905. This could almost be a different country, let alone a different period, for the magnificent elm trees which were dotted in the hedgerows and were the most significant of land-marks, providing shelter, fuel and lumber, have almost disappeared from the local scene following the outset of Dutch Elm Disease in the 1970s. The men who worked the farms, labouring nearly all the daylight hours in summer, were a special breed who often tended their large allotments in their spare time to make "ends meet" for their families. It should be remembered also that the Sabbath day of rest was rigidly observed, so spare time was in very short supply. Note the large patch in the seat of the man's trousers. This was typical at this time, as all working garments were repaired over and over again. When they could no longer be repaired they were not discarded, as the material was kept for future repairs, and the buttons, together with hooks and eyes, were carefully removed and stored in the "button tin" that every family had.

225.   Haymakers on Mr. Peter Goss's (Glebe) farm, *circa* 1910. *Left to right*: W. Roads, "Pete" Goss, "Willie" Creed, T. Franks, E. Dormer. The men look fairly fresh, but for the horse it appears to have been a long day!

226.   Another photograph of haymakers, once again probably on Glebe Farm. It was common practice for farmers to employ casual labour at busy hay-making and harvest times, and also to team up with neighbouring farms. *Left to right*: "Willie" Creed, Reg Sharp, —, W. Roads. *Front row*: F. Dormer, E. Dormer, "Pete" Goss, —. Of particular interest is the earthenware beer flagon in its protective basket, and the hobnailed boots of the two boys.

227.   At the centre of this photograph is Mr. Tom Goss the village saddler and harness maker, whilst on the right is Aubrey Dennis. Mr. Goss's workshop was situated next door to Price's shop in the High Street, from where he provided an essential service in this rural self-sufficient community. Photograph *circa* 1900.

228.   The well-dressed Edwardian child is epitomised in this study of "Will" and Margaret Franks in their Sunday best around 1910. Photographed in Albert Cherry's studio, as were the vast majority of the photographs of this type in Waddesdon.

229.   Pillow lace-making had been an important cottage industry to the rural communities of Bucks for over 100 years. However, the advent of machinery and cheap foreign imports had reduced this art to a local curiosity by the 1920s. Here we see five ladies who must have known pillow lace-making in its heyday, when many females in the locality toiled for long hours to earn a few extra shillings. *Left to right*: Mrs. K. Cripps, Mrs. Phillips, —, Mrs. P. Atkins, Mrs. Fields. As can be seen, the lace is produced on a "pillow" which is in fact a tightly encased pack of straw.

230.   In this photograph Mrs. Polly Hicks stands in the doorway of her cottage at the edge of Gullatt's Furlong on the Aylesbury Road. A tiny cottage by modern standards, but a comfortable home for Mr. and Mrs. Hicks and their family of four boys in 1910. All houses built during this period had solid walls (i.e. not cavity), but this and the adjoining cottage were the only examples in the village where the bricks were laid on edge.

231.   Unlike many other model villages which were established around this period, Waddesdon's population consisted of the normal spread, including of course a proportion who may have experienced only a few years of the relative prosperity of the new village. This photograph is of Mr. and Mrs. Biswell, *circa* 1900. They lived in the Rothschild cottage opposite Princes Lodge, Silk Street. Staunch Wesleyans, they were related to John Biswell, long-time superintendent of the Sunday School, whose memorial plaque is mounted in the old chapel.

The Waddesdon Parish Magazine.

THE HARVEST FESTIVAL.

In accordance with the announcement in last month's Magazine, our Annual Festival was held on the 23rd ult. We were very fortunate in having a fine day. There was a large attendance in the Rectory grounds, but by no means so large as usual, as, unfortunately, Aylesbury Harvest Festival took place on the same day, consequently we missed very many of our Aylesbury friends who generally are present : only on one occasion since 1867 has the attendance been smaller, and then the day was very wet. It is much to be regretted (for the sake of the Infirmary) that Aylesbury made the great mistake of altering their day to ours. Under 500 people partook of tea in the large tent, and a better tea no one could wish for. Great praise is due to Messrs. Cockerell, James Goss, W. Welsh, J. Fowler, Mrs. Burnard, and the willing band of bread and cake cutters, waiters, and tray holders whose untiring efforts ensured such a pleasant tea party. Some half dozen tray holders, however, failed to put in an appearance at the last moment, and their vacant places caused some inconvenience, and exposed the Rector to some disagreeable remarks from two or three ill-conditioned visitors. We append the list of 2/6 donors : it is to be regretted that their number in so marked a manner decreases :—

CONTRIBUTORS OF 2/6 TRAYS.

Adams, Miss	Field, Mrs.	Quartley, Mrs.
Alcock, Mrs.	Field, Mr., Aylesbury	Reader, Mr.
Belgrove, Mr.	Fowler, Mrs. J.	Ridgway, Mrs. (2)
Belgrove, Mrs.	Franklin, Mr.	Robbins, Mrs.
Biggs, Mrs.	Franklin, Mrs. W.	Rose, Mr.
Bliss, Mr. (2)	Friends Two, Aylesbury 3/6	Saunders, Mrs. L.
Bliss, Mrs. R.	Friend, A	Sims, Mr. (2)
Bradford, Mr.	Gibbs, Mr. R., Aylesbury	Sims, Mrs.
Broad, Mrs.	Goss, Mrs. James	Stornell, Mrs.
Bulford, Mr. (2)	Goss, Mrs. John	Strong, Mr.
Burnard, Mrs.	Goss, Miss Ellen	Strong, Miss
Cannon, Mr. T.	Goss, Mrs. T. G.	Tack, Mr. Stephen
Clare, Mr.	Goss, Miss S. J.	Taylor, Mr., Aylesbury
Clark, Mrs. (2) L. Winchendon	Goss, Mrs. Joseph	Taylor, Mr.
Clark, Mr., Aylesbury	Griffin, Mrs. John	Thorne, Mrs. G.
Cleaver, Mrs.	Holt, Mrs., Sharp's Hill	Tinsley, Mrs.
Cockerell, Mrs.	Kibble, Mr. J. (2)	Tompkins, The late Mrs.
Cooper, Mr. George	King, Mrs. O.	Treadwell, Mrs. John
Cooper, Mrs. (2)	Macdona, Rev. G. V.	Treadwell, The Misses
Cooper, Miss, sen.	Marriott, Mrs.	Uff, Mrs.
Copcutt, Mrs. T.	Mason, Mrs.	Varney, Mrs. W.
Cripps, Mrs. T.	Matthews, Mrs. (2)	Ward, Mr. George
Cripps, Mrs. John	Mumford, Mr. J. A.	Watson, Mrs. Horace
Crook, Mrs. Edwin	Monk, Mr. (2)	Webb, Mr.
Crook, Mrs. John	Monk, Miss	Welsh, Mrs.
Crook, Mrs. Levi	Palmer, Mr.	Wheelton, Mrs.
Curtis, Miss	Page, Mrs.	Wilcox, Mr.
Dodwell, Mrs. (2)	Payne, Mrs.	Williams, Rev. T. J. (2)
Fisher, Mr. W.	Payne, Mr. S. G.	Williams, Miss
Flowers, Mr. (4)	Poulton, Mr., Aylesbury	Woods, Mrs.

The fruit, flower, and vegetable show was very good, but there were hardly as many exhibitors as we expected. Our Honorary Secretary, Mr. Quartley, was, as heretofore, indefatigable in his labours throughout the day. The judges, who most efficiently discharged their difficult task, were Messrs. Anstiss, of Brill, and Smith, of Wotton House Gardens, who both brought handsome specimens of plants to adorn the tent. The following were the awards :—

232. This fascinating report from the October 1880 Parish Magazine provides a wealth of information on the recreation in Waddesdon at that time. The long-established harvest festival had become an important event in the village calendar with large numbers involved in the preparation and the activities of the day. The proceeds had always been donated to Aylesbury Infirmary. As in all rural areas the cultivation of allotments and cottage gardens was the most common pass-time in Waddesdon, and for the majority the growing of all kinds of vegetables and even wheat was seen as an essential part of life.

The Waddesdon Parish Magazine.   39

Fruit.—Cooking Apples : 1, P. Dodwell ; 2, J. Cripps ; 3, G. Cannon. Dessert Apples : 1, J. Crook ; 2, Mrs. Dennis ; 3, F. Cripps. Pears : 1 R. Coles ; 2, W. Alcock. Plums : 1, A. Shepherd ; 2, J. Syratt. Damsons : 1, J. Syratt ; 2, P. Dodwell. Grapes : 1, R. Coles ; 2, F. Cripps.

Flowers.—Geraniums : 1, W. Welsh ; 2, Mr. Evans ; 3, Mrs. Franklin. Fuschias : 1. Mrs. Stagg ; 2, Mrs. Evans ; 3, Mrs Stagg. Any other Variety : 1. Mrs. Thorne ; 2, C. Samworth ; 3, Mr. Webb. Musk : Emma Clark. Pansies : Mrs. Syratt. Asters : Mrs. Syratt. Creeper : 1, Miss S. Treadwell ; 2, J. Griffin. Memorial Device : 1, Miss Matthews. Hand Bouquet : 1, Mrs. Figg ; 2, Miss A. Treadwell ; 3, H. Herring. Special Winchendon Prize (Rev. J. Howe) : Emma Rodwell. Collection of Wild Flowers (Church Sunday School Children) : 1, S. Olliffe ; 2, E. Keen ; 3, E. Varney. Collection of Wild Flowers (open) : R. Mumford. Cut Flowers : A. Fenn. Button Hole Bouquet : L. Coles.

Vegetables.—Potatoes (White Kidneys) : 1, J. Timms ; 2, F. Evans ; 3, W. Welsh, (Red Kidneys) : 1, W. Evans, junr. ; 2, W. Ewers ; 3, T. Keedle. (White Rounds) : 1, W. Welsh ; 2, W. Evans, junr. ; 3. W. Welsh. (Red Rounds) : 2, Joseph Andrews. Turnips : 1, Thomas Fowler ; 2, W. Keen ; 3, C. Humphrey. Carrots (Long) : 1, W. Keen ; 2, H. Craker ; (Intermediate) : 1, W. Welsh. (Short, : 1, W. Keen ; 2, Wheelton. Parsnips : 1, S. Roads ; 2, A. Atkins. Onions : 1, A. Atkins ; 2, H. Turner ; 3, W. Keen. Kidney Beans : J. Dymock. Scarlet Runners : 1, J. Spaul ; 2, S. Roads ; 3, E. Cannon. Peas : 1, S. Page. Vegetable Marrows : 1, J. Syratt ; 2, H. Herring. Collection of Marrows : 1, F. Evans. Cucumbers (Ridge) 1, J. Franklin ; 2, F. Evans. Celery : 1, H. Craker ; 2, F. Evans ; 3, C. Turner. Savoys : 1, W. Welsh ; 2, C. Turner ; 3, E. Pollard. Cabbages : 1, J. Franks ; 2, W. Crook ; 3, W. Ewers. Red Cabbages : 1, T. Field ; 2, Ford. Winter Greens : 1, J. Franks ; 2, D. Higgins ; 3, S. Cripps ; Basket of Vegetables : 1, W. Welsh.

There were, for the first time, Athletic Sports in connection with the Festival. These were very popular ; they took place in the home close. The Programme comprised eight events, and all were well filled. Mr. Cockerell was starter ; Messrs. Simms and Lindsay, judges, and Mr. Tinsley, secretary. We add the results.

100 Yards Handicap Race. 1, A Tankard, W. Simms (Aylesbury) ; 2, Meerschaum Pipe, W. Alcock.

Throwing at the Wicket. 1, Cricket Bat, F. D. Cripps ; 2, Belt, McKernan.

400 Yards Flat Race (Handicap). 1, Carriage Clock, North (Aylesbury) ; 2, Flask, Griffin.

Boys' Race (under 16). 1, Butter Dish, Cannon (Quainton) ; 2, Knife, H. Alcock ; 3, Clock, T. Cripps.

200 Yards Handicap Hurdle Race (10 flights). 1, Tea Pot ; 2, Marmalade Dish ; a dead heat between North and Parkinson, stakes divided.

Three-legged Race. 1, Globe Lamp, H. Alcock ; 2, ditto, R. Parkinson.

Girls' Race (30 entries). 1, Cruet Stand, F. Buckle ; 2, Umbrella, M. Biswell ; 3, Scarf, J. Cripps.

Bumping Match in Sacks. 1, Clock, W. Alcock ; 2, Lamp, H. Saunders.

The Prizes were distributed by Miss Williams, for whom hearty cheers were given. The Waddesdon brass band, as in former years, gave their services, and played in very good style. During the afternoon numbers found their way to the old Church, and expressed admiration for the beautiful decorations. During the three days preceding the festival, many fair hands were engaged in the work ; the willing band included Miss Williams, the Misses Cooper, Treadwell, E. and S. J. Goss, Matthews, Mason, Woods, Mrs. Quartley, Mrs. King, Miss Strong, Miss Custerson, Misses Biswell, Fenn, Stonnell, Messrs. Quartley, Sayer, Tinsley, Goss, Payne, and the Rev. G. V. Macdona ; a full, fair, and highly complimentary account of the decorations is given in the Herald. The services were Holy Communion at 8 a.m., and full Evensong at 6.15 p.m. The congregation was not as large as usual, and the collection was comparatively small, £4 12s. 10¾d. The Service was well rendered ; Mr. Macdona sang the Prayers, the Lessons were read by the Rev. R. H. Pigott and E. R. Iremonger : a suitable sermon was preached by the Rev. Thomas Ivens, Vicar of Piddington, Oxon, the text Heb. vi. 7-8 ; the Choir was very large, and the singing unusually good :

The average amount of land per allotment holder in Waddesdon during the 1870s was around 40 poles. The Allotment Society became a prominent organisation in the community, providing members with cheap seed potatoes, soot for darkening and improving the soil, and the supply of pea and bean sticks. Their annual sports and horticultural show in the cricket field on August Monday became a popular attraction for crowds from far and wide and as many of the exhibitors were men employed on the Manor gardens it is not surprising that the standards in the shows were very high.

233.   For the young men in the area, one of the popular benefits arising from a grand house in the parish was the influx of young ladies employed "in service". Here we have a charming study by Albert Cherry of two such girls at a footpath stile, *circa* 1910. The girl on the right is Miss Pratt, who proved in photograph no. 195 that she was capable of making heads turn in more ways than one.

234.   Mounted troops on army manoeuvres passing the lime tree which stood by Grace's shop at the Quainton Road junction with the High Street. For some years until the outbreak of war in August 1914, summer exercises involving elements of the regular and reserve forces were held on the Waddesdon estate.

235.   Troops and horses resting near the Arthur Goodwin Almshouses whilst on manoeuvres in the locality. It was ironic for many of these men, who were trained in horsemanship and the warfare of movement, that when it came, the Great War was largely fought from the trenches and of course on foot. When these manoeuvres were held in the area the camps were usually pitched in Butchers Piece and Banky Ground near Warmstone, and at The Great Butts (The Big Field) at Westcott.

236.   A detachment of field artillery heads past the village green towards Aylesbury, whilst in the opposite direction comes a detachment of mounted soldiers. These scenes in rural Bucks in 1912 no doubt provided everyone with an interesting diversion at a seemingly idyllic period in our history. No one could have imagined the horrors awaiting the participants in the Great War just a few short months away, nor the special significance that this piece of village green would hold in the decades to come.

237.   The Empire supported the Allied cause from the outset
and large numbers of colonial troops visited this country *en
route* for the Western Front or other theatres of war. Here we
see the son of Mr. and Mrs. Walker, emigrants to Brisbane,
Australia, in the mid 1870s, visiting relatives Mrs. K. Cripps
and Mrs. C. Fowler.

237.   The Great War was perceived by the vast majority
as a fight against aggressors, for it was as a result of
Germany's invasion of neutral Belgium that Great Britain
declared war. This photograph of George Gurney from
Upper Winchendon shows us a confident young artillery-
man who until he enlisted had been happily employed as
a farm worker. His skills with animals were put to good
use in caring for the teams of horses which pulled the
heavy gun limber, and with his gun battery George saw
considerable action on the Western Front. He survived
the war but returned to his farm work with vivid
memories of mud and devastation in the Battle of the
Somme, and physical reminders of twice being the victim
of mustard gas attacks.

239.   During the Great War women were employed in all manner of work previously considered as being in the male province; however, in rural areas wives and daughters had always helped with the hay-making. It is the location which brings home the message in this photograph. The shortage of fodder must have been extreme indeed to persuade the Estate to curtail cricketing activities and to grow hay on Waddesdon's fine field, *circa* 1917. The man is George Styles and the ladies include Nell Rolf, Mrs. Atkins, Mrs. Rhodes, May Marlow and Mrs. Gale.

240.   Those men and women who "kept the home fires burning" were constantly active in fund-raising schemes which were intended to alleviate the suffering of the war casualties. The Red Cross had a prominent role to play in this work and was well supported in Waddesdon. On the occasion of this photograph the donkey had recently been auctioned in aid of the Red Cross. In fact it was bought several times, then given back and re-auctioned until it had realised a total of £54.6s.0d. (probably £1,500 at 1995 prices).

241.   The people of Waddesdon had a long tradition of gardening to provide a large proportion of their own food. However, the situation created by the war compelled the more than usual enrolment of schoolboys in work normally done by adults. This photograph of around 1918 shows boys from the British School ready to tend their plots in the school gardens. *Back row*: Stan Fowler, Don Carter, Ernie Biswell, Eddie Dymock. *Middle row*: Leslie Cripps, Fred George, Bernard Cripps, Dick Fowler, Percy Sharp, Tom Biswell. *Front row*: Bert Walker, George Fowler, Jack Biswell, Wally Carter.

242.   On 30 March 1916 an extremely violent storm caused much damage in the area. The Wilderness at Upper Winchendon was particularly hard hit, as can be seen from this photograph taken the next day. Perhaps not such bad news for those allowed to take the wood home! Note how the photographer has posed all the workers.

243.   Jack Rolfe joined the colours at the outbreak of war in August 1914, and by 1916 at the age of 19 had gained the distinction of being the youngest Company Sergeant Major in the British Army. He served with the 2nd Bucks Battalion of the Oxford and Bucks Light Infantry during the whole of its existence during the Great War, seeing active service on the Western Front from 1916–1918. In this photograph he is seated in the centre of the picture. Note the Bucks Battalion cap badge. On 9 July 1917, C.S.M. J. H. Rolfe was awarded the Distinguished Conduct Medal "For conspicuous gallantry and devotion to duty". The D.C.M. was also awarded to another Waddesdonian, Lou Radwell. Both Jack and Lou survived the war that had taken the lives of so many of their pals, and Jack resumed where he had left off in local football, becoming something of a legend in the Waddesdon colours.

244.   The studio of Albert Cherry saw a steady procession during the war years of village families who wished to send their loved ones a memento to be carried on their travels. These two photographs are typical of many which Mr. Cherry produced. 244 shows Mrs. Louisa Cripps with three of her six children, Annie, Joe, and Doris. Of her elder children, May was "away in service" and Harry and Frank were with the 2nd Bucks Battalion on the Western Front.

245.   Mrs. Christine Atkins and Mary Annie May (wife and daughter of 43125 Private William E. Atkins who served with the Devon Regiment).

246. Rejected on physical fitness grounds at his first attempt to enlist in the Oxford and Bucks Light Infantry, Harry Cripps carried out physical training to improve his fitness and re-applied. He was accepted and posted to the 2nd Bucks Battalion to serve alongside many other Waddesdon men. A keen member the Waddesdon "Old Band", Harry continued his hobby with the Battalion Band. On July 30 1917, the 3rd Battle of Ypres commenced. This long-drawn-out offensive was to last for more than three months and cost the Allies and their German enemy each 250,000 casualties. Just a small element of that battle involved the 2nd Bucks Battalion and at 4.45 am on 22 August they advanced as part of a large assault force of several infantry brigades. The conditions were appalling and the defenders well organised, but despite heavy losses some objectives were secured. The battalion had mustered 13 officers and 637 other ranks for the attack, but by the evening 11 officers and 338 men were reported as casualties. Of these, 7 officers and 113 men were confirmed as killed, including from Waddesdon Sergeant H. Carter, L. Cpl. R. Bird, L. Cpl. H. Biswell, Pte. H. Cripps, Pte. S. Stonehill, and Pte. W. Thorp. As with so many killed in that war, no trace was ever found of Harry Cripps.

247.   Armistice Day 1918. The almost spontaneous procession of sundry servicemen and villagers making their way to a thanksgiving at the Parish Church, is recorded by the camera of Miss Elsie Turnham from outside the Five Arrows Hotel.

248.   During and immediately after the war, at the far end of Queen Street beyond the Gardens and Bothy there was a camp for the containment of German prisoners of war. These P.O.W.s were secured in the compound under armed guard when not employed on local farms and forestry work. By all accounts they were rather glad to be out of active service and appreciated the outdoor life and good food which regularly rewarded their efforts. Following action on the Western Front, Tom Carr was posted to Waddesdon as a P.O.W. guard and daily marched his charges down the High Street on their way to Sheepcote Hill. Once off the main road at Warmstone, one prisoner would take his pack whilst another would take his rifle, and they would proceed up the hill towards Cat Lane, singing as they went. This photograph is of the P.O.W. camp choir, taken about the time of their departure home in 1919. As they proceeded down Waddesdon High Street for the last time they serenaded the villagers with a German lullaby which caused more than a few tears of farewell.

HARRY CRIPPS

249 and 250. Grateful officials and grieving relatives did their best to commemorate the service and sacrifice of those who had died and those who had survived as combatants in the Great War. The gun-metal medallion was to become a treasured reminder of a son who lay somewhere to the west of Passchendaele and the certificate issued to each returning serviceman officially recorded the feelings of those who now welcomed them home.

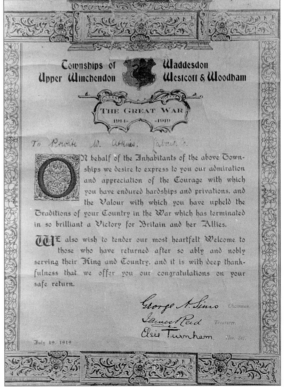

Townships of   Waddesdon
Upper Winchendon   Westcott & Woodham

THE GREAT WAR
1914   1919

To Private W. Atkins, Watcott.

On behalf of the Inhabitants of the above Townships we desire to express to you our admiration and appreciation of the Courage with which you have endured hardships and privations, and the Valour with which you have upheld the Traditions of your Country in the War which has terminated in so brilliant a Victory for Britain and her Allies.

We also wish to tender our most heartfelt Welcome to those who have returned after so ably and nobly serving their King and Country, and it is with deep thankfulness that we offer you our congratulations on your safe return.

George N. Sims, Chairman
James Reid, Treasurer
Alice Turnham, Hon. Sec.

July 19, 1919.

251.   Communities throughout the world now set about raising memorials to the fallen, and Waddesdon was no exception. A fund-raising committee was formed, chaired by the Rector, the Rev. Farmer, with other officials representing all denominations in the village. The target was £450 and a wide range of money-raising activities were organised. In the photograph we have Connie Owen, whose part in a variety concert is described in the accompanying *Bucks Herald* report.

VARIETY ENTERTAINMENT.—On Thursday week a large audience assembled at the Waddesdon Hall, patronising an entertainment given by members and friends of the Wesleyan Young People's Society, in aid of the Parish War Memorial. The curtain rose on a child (Connie Owen) dressed as a fairy, who opened the evening by bidding everyone "Welcome." The child looked very pretty in her fairy dress, and the audience loudly applauded her little recitation. A long and interesting programme followed, each item being thoroughly enjoyed. Songs were rendered by Mesdames Crook, Herald, and Newell, Mr. Adamson (who was accompanied by Miss Tattam), and Mr. Gordon Biswell. The pianists, Miss A. Taylor and Miss D. Judd, ably accompanied the singing. Recitations were rendered by Mrs. Littlechild and Mr. C. Taylor. During the evening the children of the Sunday School sang action songs, which were well received. A musical sketch, entitled "Matrimonee," given by members, caused much laughter, as did the farce, "The Haunted Room," which completed the programme. The financial result, £25:0:10, was most gratifying.

252.   By late March 1921 the memorial was ready for its dedication and unveiling ceremony. On Easter Sunday 27 March this commenced with a parade of ex-servicemen, led by the remnants of the Old Prize and Temperance Band. In this photograph the parade is approaching the old Square or Green, where appropriately the memorial had been sited on Waddesdon's last remaining patch of common land. The ancient hub of the village would now be preserved for ever, in the memory of all Waddesdon's fallen

253.   Over a hundred ex-servicemen paraded in the charge of Mr. A. Sirett, whilst the band played and the crowd gathered. The War Memorial is draped in the Union Jack awaiting the official unveiling to be carried out by Major General Sir Robert Fanshawe.

WADDESDON.
WAR MEMORIAL UNVEILED.

A large Cornish granite cross, set on a massive base, and approached by a three-step platform commemorates the men of Waddesdon parish who laid down their lives in the Great War. Sixty-two names are inscribed thereon, and the front of the base records that the memorial is erected —

To the Glory of God and in proud and grateful remembrance of the men of Waddesdon who gave their lives in the Great War 1914—1919.
Faithful unto death.
Their name liveth for evermore.

The large number of names chiselled out of the side panels emphasised the heavy toll of young manhood which the War made upon the village, the inhabitants of which have every reason to regard with sorrowful pride the permanently recorded roll of honour which now occupies one of the most commanding positions by the side of the main road, near the Hall.

The memorial was unveiled on Easter Sunday by Major-Gen. Sir Robert Fanshawe, who referred, very appropriately, to the services rendered by the 1st Bucks Battalion when serving in France in a division of which he had the command. The mention he made of small but relatively large and important duties undertaken by one element of the Services applied with equal point to the vast number of other units represented on the roll of honour, and in the large company present at the unveiling. Rev. J. E. G. Farmer (rector of Waddesdon), conducted the dedication service, assisted by Rev. J. Williams (Wesleyan minister, Aylesbury Circuit), who read the Lesson. Waddesdon Old and Waddesdon Temperance Bands, combined (under the conductorship of Mr. S. C. Camp), led the singing of the hymns "O God our Help in ages past," "For all the Saints," and "Through the night of doubt and sorrow," and two trumpeters from No. 4 Section, R.A.F., Halton (A. Smart, Aberdeen, and H.

254. Cutting from the *Bucks Herald*, 2 April 1921.

255.   The War Memorial was dedicated by the Rector, the Rev. J. E. G. Farmer, who had, like many of those taking part, his own personal sadness in the proceedings, for his son Henry was amongst the 62 names inscribed in the base of the granite cross. Here we see the closely-packed crowd which had formed around the War Memorial (and hardly a bare head in sight). At "The Roses" across the High Street can be seen several ladies in the porch, whilst from the bedroom windows two maids are determined to witness the occasion.

256. The War Memorial, new and without the perimeter enclosure which was added when funds allowed. At the base are spread the floral tributes which were placed after the unveiling and dedication ceremony.

257. Mr. Ben Thorne, shown here outside his premises in the High Street, opposite the Primitive Methodist Chapel, started Waddesdon's first motor-bus service. In the early 1920s he provided a regular service on Wednesdays and Saturdays, using "The Waddesdon Queen" driven by Mr. Percy Goss (at the wheel in this photograph). The bus was based upon a Model T Ford and one of its first engagements was ferrying Waddesdon's football team and supporters to the Oving Village Cup Final. The trip to Aylesbury cost 6d. (2½p) single and 10d. (4p approx) for a return ticket. Children were carried at a reduced rate. The Waddesdon Queen lasted only a few years. It overheated and caught fire near the windmill on the Aylesbury road and was damaged beyond repair. The business premises are still in use, but now accommodate an Italian restaurant (1995).

[handwritten invoice:]

22

Mr. Richardson.   The House

1922.

Feb 21.   Repairs to mrs Rothschild's
           Bath Chair. Rebuilding
           Front Wheel. fitting new Axle
           Boring out side Wheel Hubs.
           making new Steel Axle for same
           & fitting 3 new Cushion tyres
           Painting Lining & Varnishing   8 10 -
      23. Supplying 12 doz Refills for
           fire Extinguishers   1 12 -
                    Paid By Cheque
                         march 1922.   £   10   2 -

258.   Whenever running repairs of a mechanical nature were required in the vicinity, people invariably called upon the services of David Evans. The Manor and Estate were no exception. In early 1922 when Miss Alice was already in need of a Bath-chair, the extensive repairs itemised on this invoice were carried out by David Evans, for the princely sum of £8. 10s. 0d. (£8.50p). The final item, 12 dozen refills for fire extinguishers, indicates another aspect of the services provided from the Evans business premises.

259.   In common with many other large private enterprises, Waddesdon had its own volunteer Fire Brigade. Essentially employed to carry out fire prevention and fire fighting for the Manor and Estate, they also provided fire fighting services for the locality. This photograph of around 1925 shows the crew of the station handcart carrying out practice drill under the watchfull eye of Fire Officer Tom Goss.

260.   Members of the Waddesdon Estate Fire Brigade, *circa* 1925. *Standing left to right*: Jack Uff (Estate), Tom Evans (Coal Merchant), Len Cook (Butcher), Randall Styles (Newsagent), Baden Roads (Barber), Len Walton (Estate). *Sitting left to right*: G. Cannon (Baker), Tommy Franklin (Grocer), Tom Goss (Sadler), Edwin Harris (Schoolmaster), Arthur Hicks (Gravedigger, etc.), Frank Wheeler (Driver).

261.   James de Rothschild, like the Baron, was a member of the Liberal Party and was destined to become a Member of Parliament. In the 1920s Waddesdon Estate was the venue for huge fêtes in aid of Liberal Party funds. Those attending would be addressed by renowned politicians, including on one occasion none other than David Lloyd George. This, before the advent of radio and television, was a rare experience for most people. The side-show pictured above harks back to the First World War cartoon character "Old Bill", and illustrates the efforts which were made to impress the supporters of the fête. The "Tommy" lounging at the dug-out doorway is Sam Court.

262.   The years following the Great War were difficult for many people and there was a great need for charitable action to assist those who had fallen on hard times. This photograph of 1925 shows a charabanc-load of children outside the British School in Baker Street having returned from an egg collecting tour of local farms, etc. The eggs were then delivered to the Royal Bucks Hospital in Aylesbury.

263.   Mr. and Mrs. James de Rothschild regularly entertained their guests at Waddesdon. In this photograph we see the Princess Royal being greeted by the schoolchildren of the village at the entrance to the Manor grounds, next to the Reading Room, *circa* 1925. The following year King George V and Queen Mary paid a private visit, and at intervals important politicians such as Mr. Asquith and Mr. Churchill, past and future Prime Ministers respectively, came to enjoy the hospitality, perhaps play golf, visit the stud farm, and walk around the extensive gardens which continued to meet the exacting standards of the past.

264. By 1925 village life in Waddesdon had settled down to a familiar pattern. The village traditions and customs were still enjoyed in much the same way as pre-war, and for the time being the villagers were not greatly affected by events elsewhere. In this photograph, the Cricket Pavilion is once again used to present a group of Waddesdon (Methodist) Sunday School members, perhaps on the occasion of their annual Treat. A strong community spirit prevailed and most of the organisations such as this were destined for many future years of success.

265. The infants and Class Two pupils of the Church of England (National) School around 1925. By all accounts school-life was rather more fun than the straight faces would have us believe. *Back row left to right*: Miss Harrison, T. Munday, J. Radwell, W. Dennis, T. Brown, G. Martin, Mr. E. Harris, A. Hedges, I. Read, R. Carter, M.Eldridge, A. Munday, Miss Read. *Second row*: T. Munday, E. Read, C. Read, L. George, D. Eldridge, F. Slade, H. Pitts, P. Jeeves, J. Biswell, M. Dennis, H. Goss, M. Slade. *Third row*: N. Franks, V. Burgess, V. Sirett, D. Hinton, F. Brackley, J. Bishop, R. Harms, J. Wicks, R. Webb, H. Franks, V. Biswell, M. Butler. *Front row*: G. Biswell, P. George, R. Evans, L. Holland, S. Atkins, L. Wood, D. Sirett, W. Jones, M. Cannon, L. Goss.

WADDESDON IN 1995

During the past 70 years Waddesdon has retained much of the structure established a century ago. Despite the addition of several local authority housing estates and the infill by private housing of many closes and gardens, the village seems remarkably unaltered to those who live here. Some landmarks have unfortunately gone, and new ones have become part of the normal scene. The "Rothschild end" of the village has enjoyed the benefits of a good idea well executed, and visually will spring few surprises upon a returning exile. Likewise Lodge Hill, for the Manor and surrounding parkland has undergone a renaissance of impressive proportions, providing the perspectives of a hundred years ago, yet incorporating the latest technology and innovation. Rather similar to the circumstances in 1895!

The Manor however, perhaps inevitably, was the subject of the most momentous change, when on the death of Mr. James de Rothschild in 1957, it was bequeathed to the National Trust together with its contents and 160 acres of surrounding grounds. Subsequently both Mrs. Dorothy de Rothschild, until her death in 1988, and Lord Jacob Rothschild, her cousin and heir, have successively maintained a strong and active association with the Manor. The recent renovation work is one example of the benefits of that association.

Whilst the village has reassuringly retained most of its physical attributes, its role has changed along with the lifestyle of its inhabitants. The Manor and Estate still employ more persons within the village than others, but the majority of us travel beyond the parish boundaries for our work, provisions and entertainment.

Social life has changed dramatically; sports clubs and other organisations cater for a wider range of members than those of yester-year. Cultural groups struggle to survive, brass bands, the Philharmonic Society and other music makers are long gone, the Reading Rooms and the Institute too. Most families do not have an allotment, for it is no longer a necessity of life, and vegetables are giving way to grass and flowers in cottage gardens. Although the population is around 2,000 as in the year 1900, a much higher proportion is transient and has few previous links with Waddesdon.

The High Street still forms part of the A41 trunk road, but the modern traffic volumes cause problems for those living adjacent to this ancient thoroughfare. This problem has been one of the few unifying factors in the community in recent years.

All in all, Waddesdon is still a very pleasant village in which to reside; this is reflected in the price of housing, which is marginally higher than in neighbouring villages. Visitors and villagers alike enjoy the many local walks and views, the fine wide High Street, the well-maintained properties, and savour some of the nineteenth century model village qualities which were implanted a hundred years ago.

The first six photographs illustrating this section are contemporary aerial views of the village and they can be compared with those taken in 1931 and included in the section on the New Village. The captions will draw attention to major differences, but the full story of post-1925 Waddesdon is beyond the scope of this book.

Finally, it is a pleasant coincidence that our book can be brought to a close by recording the third visit to Waddesdon Manor of the reigning monarch in little over 100 years. On 31 March 1995 Her Majesty Queen Elizabeth and His Royal Highness Prince Phillip paid a private visit as guests of Lord and Lady Rothschild, to mark the completion of the final phase of the restoration programme on the Manor and to carry out the official opening ceremony of the Sèvres Gallery.

The six photographs at the end of this section record the Manor, the welcoming villagers, and the arrival of the Queen and Prince Phillip on this auspicious day.

266.   When this photograph viewing Waddesdon from the South is compared with no.150, we have an overall impression of a much denser settlement, with many small housing developments infilling where closes, orchards and gardens were previously tended. In the foreground the Church School has gone, and nearby Grove Way has long since appended to Baker Street. At the north-east extremity lies the relatively new Glebe Farm, replacing both the old Manor of the Third Portion (Atte Green), and also the previous Glebe Farm which stood alongside the Quainton Road.

267.   If one compares this photograph with no. 151, the nearside outline is remarkably unchanged. Looking closer, the mill chimney and the gasometer have both gone from the end of Quainton Road, though more than 60 years separate their removals. On the far side (eastern periphery) of the village, large housing developments have altered the profile and extended the boundary a few hundred yards towards Aylesbury. In the upper right corner of this view the school complex and the Bail farm buildings are both easily distinguished.

268.   This photograph illustrates the twists and turns taken by the High Street, and shows quite clearly the outline followed by Waddesdon's mediaeval by-pass which is traced by the hedgerows at the lower Parson's Close and Fennimore Home Ground, on the left of picture. This photograph can be compared with no. 152.

269.   A view from the south, again showing a much denser concentration of housing, but thankfully no significant development in the nearside of the photograph. However, to be mourned by tree lovers is the demise of all the elm trees which marked the ancient hedge-lines both in the village and in the surrounding countryside and more recently the felling of various magnificent coniferous trees which distinguished the Manor Estate plantations at the base of Lodge Hill. See photograph no. 153.

270.   Waddesdon from the east. An opportunity to pick out a few elements not easily visible from other viewpoints, in particular the profile of Baker Street and the modern development at the old Council School. Down in the right foreground is Little Britain and on the left of picture is the ancient field Golden Nob, for many years an allotment field, but for how much longer?

271.   A great deal of fairly new development can be observed in this fine view of Waddesdon from the south-east. In the left foreground is the large complex of buildings and sports facilities associated with the County Combined and Church of England Secondary Schools. In the top left corner of this photograph the newly renovated Dairy, now a Conference Centre, and beyond that the modern green-houses on the Estate can be discerned. Rectory Drive, Little Britain, Chestnut Close and Baron's Court are visible, superimposed amongst the network of roads and tracks which formed the village of more than one hundred years ago.

272.   A comprehensive restoration programme of the Manor, which included extensive roof replacement, was carried out under the auspices of Lord Rothschild and reached its conclusion early in 1995. In addition a new gallery for the display of Sèvres porcelain had been completed. To mark this occasion, on Friday 31 March 1995, Her Majesty Queen Elizabeth and His Royal Highness Prince Phillip made a private visit to the Manor as guests of Lord and Lady Rothschild. Local villagers were invited to witness this occasion by greeting the Royal party at the North Front of the Manor. Here we see a goodly crowd gathering about half an hour before the arrival time.

273.   A section of the crowd, flags and all, cheerfully passing the time before 11.00 am, when the Royal party was due to arrive.

274. A practice wave for the photographer from pupils of Waddesdon County Combined School. (Photograph © *Bucks Herald*.)

275. A view of the South Front of the Manor on the occasion of the Royal visit, showing the Royal Standard flying on the flag-staff. It is no coincidence the appearance is identical with that of 100 years ago, as great care in the restoration work, attention to detail, and high quality craftsmanship have combined to attain the Waddesdon standard once again.

276.   The moment everyone has been awaiting. After alighting from her limousine, Her Majesty was presented with posies by numerous children, including several who were part of the official reception party and many who were not! (Photograph © *Bucks Herald*.)

277.   In the days of the Baron, Royal guests were usually invited to mark the occasion by planting a young tree in the parkland adjacent to the Manor. The tradition was resumed when the Queen and Prince Phillip each carried out this familiar task, witnessed by gardeners and other staff. This photograph shows the party *en route* to the tree planting site near Daffodil Valley. The Queen is escorted by Beth Tomassini (daughter of Lord and Lady Rothschild), Gardens Manager, preceding Prince Phillip and Lord and Lady Rothschild. (Photograph © Dan Stevens.)

Photographs nos 274 and 276 are published by kind permission of the *Bucks Herald*, and no. 277 by permission of Dan Stevens. All other photographs in this section by I. W. Gurney (1995).

ACKNOWLEDGEMENTS

The authors are indebted to the following people and organisations for their help in providing photographs, information, and advice in the compilation of this book. Inevitably there may be some omissions, and despite our checks there may also be mistakes; for these we beg the indulgence of the reader.

Although most of the photographs in the book are of good quality, there are a few of a lower standard which have been included for historical value and to illustrate important details.

The Bucks Herald, Aylesbury

Anna Eavis, National Monuments Records Centre, Swindon
Caroline Robertson, Waddesdon Manor
London Transport Museum
Moira Birks, National Monuments Records Centre, Swindon
Mrs. Angela Gilmore, Aylesbury
Mrs. Annette Webster, Waddesdon
Mrs. Caroline McLatchy, Milton Keynes
Mrs. Christine Edmunds, Westcott
Mrs. Delphi Evans, Waddesdon
Mrs. Elizabeth Khalvet, Waddesdon
Mrs. Elizabeth McLaren, Scotland
Mrs. Joy Evans, Waddesdon
Mrs. Joyce Wicks, Wing
Mrs. M. Atkins, Waddesdon
Mrs. Margaret Batchelar, Clipstone, Leighton Buzzard
Mr. "Tucker" George, Waddesdon
Mr. Alan Gurney, Leighton Buzzard, G-BAXZ Syndicate

Mr. Alistair McLaren, Quainton
Mr. and Mrs. Andrew Langton, Waddesdon
Mr. and Mrs. Will Dennis, Aylesbury
Mr. Antony Gurney, Leighton Buzzard
Mr. B. Collings, Stoke Bruerne Canal Museum
Mr. B. Quinlan, Hunting Aerofilms Ltd, Borehamwood
Mr. Cyril Gurney, Stone
Mr. Des Sharp, Waddesdon
Mr. George Hicks, Waddesdon
Mr. Gerry Warne, Waddesdon
Mr. Harold Sharp, Stoke Mandeville
Mr. Ivor Burnell, Waddesdon
Mr. J. H. Venn, Great Missenden
Mr. Jack Slade, Waddesdon
Mr. Jim Wicks, Wing
Mr. John Norris, Northampton, G-BAXZ Syndicate
Mr. Julian Hunt, and the staff of Bucks C.C. Reference Library, Aylesbury
Mr. Les Cleaver, Wing
Mr. Oliver Franklin, Waddesdon